Personal Accounts of Modern Mississippi Hauntings

GHOSTS!

Personal Accounts of Modern Mississippi Hauntings

by Sylvia Booth Hubbard

Photographs by Robert Hubbard

QRP BOOKS
Brandon, Mississippi

*The stories in this book
are dedicated to
Jessie Lee James*

*The photographs
are dedicated to
Cleo Phillips Hubbard*

Copyright © 1992 by
Sylvia and Robert Hubbard

All Rights Reserved

Designed by Barney McKee

First Printing: October, 1992
Second Printing: June, 1993
Third Printing: February, 1995
Printed in Canada

Library of Congress Cataloging-in-Publication Data

Hubbard, Sylvia Booth,
    Ghosts! : personal accounts of modern Mississippi
    hauntings / by Sylvia Booth Hubbard; photographs
      by Robert Hubbard
        p. cm.
    ISBN 0-937552-46-1 : $9.95
    1. Ghosts—Mississippi. I. Title.
      BF 1472. U6H8 1992
       133. 1'09762—dc20   92-252232
                                        CIP

Contents

List of Photographs

Foreword

"I don't believe in ghosts, but...." I wish I had counted the number of times I was told this while working on *Ghosts!* It's hard for many people to say they actually believe in ghosts; the idea of bodiless spirits flies in the face of logic and what most of us perceive as reality. But after a firm avowal of disbelief, again and again I heard the people interviewed for this book relate unfeigned experiences that defy rationalization. While many of them had tried every means of logic to "explain away" the events that had left them simply puzzled or downright terrified, they were finally left with the conclusion that the answer must lie in the supernatural. Now that's not to say they now "believe in ghosts"—they may believe in *their* ghost but they might not necessarily believe in *your* ghost.

As I traveled across Mississippi visiting the sites in this book and the people who live and work in them, I was struck by the types of people who were coming forward with their stories. From engineers to educators, from principals to pilots, the people in this book are people of substance—people who are intelligent, solid, respected members of their communities. I am very grateful to them for sharing their experiences and thereby shedding light on a subject that many are reluctant to discuss. I have tried to let them tell you their stories in their own words, and I have neither exaggerated, sensationalized, nor embroidered the stories I was told.

Before I included a story in this book, I had to be convinced the story was real. While the existence of ghosts can't be proven scientifically, I am certain that the people in this book truly believe they live with ghosts. More than once someone would be recalling a particularly terrifying experience and I would glance down to see their arms covered with goosebumps.

Researching and writing this book was a fascinating journey of discovery. Perhaps the most important discovery was that—from all across the state—people described paranormal incidents which included similar phenomena. As you read *Ghosts!*, take note of how often the following phenomena occur again and again: footsteps, crashing noises, flashing lights or other electrical disturbances, spectral figures, and voices coming from an empty room.

And now, let us begin our ghostly expedition across Mississippi. Let's start with my own story, "Hattiesburg's Haunted Studio."

S. B. H.

Hattiesburg's
Haunted Studio

THE idea for *Ghosts!* grew out of my own experiences with the supernatural. Like many Mississippians, I have always been interested in ghost stories: hair-raising tales of hauntings were a staple of spend-the-night parties with friends and of overnight visits with cousins. But the scary idea that ghosts might actually exist was mostly left to the memories of childhood—until 1975. In that year, my husband, Bob, and I bought a house on the outskirts of Hattiesburg.

We had searched for the ideal place for quite some time with no results, because our requirements were so specific. Bob had started a photographic business, but since he was still teaching at a junior college, I was the one who ran the studio on weekdays. We had begun a family and didn't want to have to take the children to day-care centers—the only solution was a house large enough to combine our home and studio for a few years...a *ghost* was not among the requirements.

Besides being large in size, the house also had to be outside the city, since Hattiesburg's zoning laws would not permit the combination of a home and business within the city limits. Also, we had to be able to afford such a house, if we could find it in the first place. We searched for over a year. Almost by chance, if there is such a thing as chance, the ideal building came our way, one that was large enough for our needs, and just barely outside the city limits.

During the time we were house hunting, Bob had a

strange dream: "I dreamed we bought a house at #2 Oak Grove Road," he said. "And even though the dream was unusual, I didn't think anything about it until I walked in the door of this house. Then it hit me—*this is the house!*" Although the house didn't have a street number at that time, it was the second house on Oak Grove Road!

The house had a 600-square-foot main room, and other rooms included a den, three bedrooms and two baths—all connected by a hall that was L-shaped. Perfect! We pounced on the deal, and within a week, the house was ours. After we signed on the dotted line, Bob went over to check the largest room's measurements before we started repainting. It was night.

"I was sitting on the floor in this empty old house with my tape measure in hand, and it was like the entire place *came alive*," Bob said. "I heard footsteps coming up the hallway...but no one was there. I *knew* something was there and I *knew* it was in the hallway, but I didn't know what it was. My gut reaction was to run...but I had no choice except to stay.

"Even though I didn't know much about the supernatural, what I *did* know was that I had every penny I owned and every penny I could borrow in this house. I came to a quick decision.

"'Look,' I appealed to whoever or whatever, 'I just paid every cent I have to buy this place. I don't have any choice; I'm going to be here a while. Can we come to some sort of accommodation? I won't bother you if you won't bother me.'"

Bob didn't have to tell me that there was something strange about our new home. There was simply no way to hide it. Unexplainable things happened all the time. Lights flashed off and on for no apparent reason. Footsteps echoed up and down the hall. A sound like rolling barrels was often heard coming from the short section of the hall. And eeriest of all, the back bedroom was usually *cold*—even in the summer.

10

Once we accepted the fact that we were living with a ghost—or ghosts (even today we aren't sure exactly how many), we tried to discover the reason. The elderly couple we bought the house from vehemently denied they had ever been aware of anything out of the ordinary. But years later, a granddaughter who had been living with them at the time we bought the house came by to visit us.

As far as we know, the granddaughter had no idea we knew the house was haunted. She stood in her old bedroom—"the cold room"—and said, "There was always something about this room that scared me. I never liked to sleep here." We could certainly understand why.

Bit by bit, with the help of our customers, we began to piece together the history of the old house. As we did, some of the things that had puzzled us were explained. We always thought it was unusual that the house had such a large front room—about twice the size of a normal living room. And it was extremely unusual for a home built in a rural area in the 1920s or 1930s to have two bathrooms. We soon found out why.

Even though the building had been used as a home for decades, it had originally been built as a "roadhouse." The large front room was used for drinking and dancing and, of course, one of the bathrooms was for men and the other for women. The other rooms were used for various activities—all probably illegal. Finding out the house was once a dance hall and bar explained one of the most puzzling phenomena that regularly occurred in the house—the sound of barrels rolling down the hall. We believe the sound is exactly what it seems—barrels—probably kegs of beer!

Some of our customers, who were former patrons of the roadhouse, filled us in on some of the details, including the house's role in upholding the morale of our fighting boys during World War II. According to them, the house was a hub of illicit activity during the war. Small outbuildings were built around the main house and used by ladies of the

*She saw the ghost of a woman turning the corner of the hall....*Hattiesburg's Haunted Studio—Hallway.

evening to ply their trade to the delight of the thousands of soldiers stationed at Camp Shelby who made regular visits in their off-hours.

During later remodeling, we found a piece of evidence that backs up our customers' memories. When the electricians began to drill through the ceiling in order to run new wiring, we discovered an older ceiling beneath it—a ceiling covered by a dark "dance hall" wallpaper speckled with gold and silver moons and stars.

Although Bob and I were uncomfortable with sharing our home and business with something definitely not of this world, we soon realized that whatever was there meant us no harm. Sometimes it could even be an advantage...like the time our air-conditioning went out in July—the cold room came in handy.

In 1978, we separated our home and business, and the phenomena slowed down but never completely stopped. Bob quit teaching and went into photography full time, and we went about our daily lives of running a business and caring for a growing family. Our ghost was something we didn't mention—not even to our families. But, as things turned out, we didn't have to. Some of them found out our secret on their own.

I don't know when we decided our ghost, or at least our main ghost, was a young woman. We just *knew*. Through the years, we have become comfortable with her. Lee, our son and older child, has never had any experiences with her other than seeing a small toy fly through the air. Shellie, our daughter, has had several experiences with her and is the only one of the four of us to have actually seen her. In fact, Shellie said, "I don't remember *not* knowing Mary." Yes, "Mary." We may know her name.

For several months I had called the ghost "Mary" in my thoughts. One day I asked Bob if he had any idea of the ghost's name. He answered, "It's funny you should ask. A few weeks ago, the name 'Mary' just popped into my head." That afternoon when Shellie came in from school, we asked, "Shellie, do you know our ghost's name?" Without hesitation she answered, "Oh, yes. *Her name is Mary Ann.*" Of course, Mary is a very common name, but still....

A few years ago, we decided to remodel the studio. From the moment we began making preparations, we noticed a definite increase in paranormal activity. The rolling barrel noises and walking intensified. Crashing sounds occurred almost every day—and the sound of crashing when camera equipment is close at hand can be very unnerving. The sounds were so common that we stopped even checking them out. We just looked at each other and said, "There they go again."

We decided that Mary knew a change was coming and she wasn't sure she'd like it. One day I was sitting on the floor in a back room packing a cardboard box. When it was full, I folded the flaps with one end underneath another in the usual "locking" method, so that it was closed completely, pushed it to my left, and began packing another.

Suddenly I heard a swishing sound at my left elbow. I glanced over just in time to see the now *open* flaps to the first box, which I had so carefully folded closed, *refolding themselves!* I stared at the box a minute in disbelief, and then softly called, "Bob, would you come back here, please?" I was definitely in the mood for living human companionship, but I think what surprised me the most was that I wasn't particularly frightened—just startled.

A few days later, we saw a small toy sail across the room. The toy (appropriately a "Star Wars" figure) flew from its resting place near a window to a spot close to the door. But after the remodeling was finished, Mary's antics slowed, and we got the definite feeling she was pleased with the results. One room we didn't touch, however, was "Mary's Room." We use it for storage.

We are convinced that Mary keeps a watchful eye on us. One day Bob had a headache and I suggested he go home while I watched the studio. He said, "No need for me to go

all the way home. There's still a bed in the storage room.
I'll go back there and rest for a few minutes."

An hour later he walked into the main room of the studio
where I was and asked, "Did you check on me while I was
resting?" "No," I said, "I never left this room."

Bob laughed, "I didn't think so. But I know Mary was
here. While I was resting, I heard footsteps walk down the
hall and heard them walk into the room. Then I felt someone standing at the foot of the bed. My eyes were closed
and I didn't open them, but I never heard the footsteps
leave. I *know* she was watching me...I could feel her presence. I guess she was just checking on me." (Well, he *had*
agreed to coexist.)

In 1990, Lee graduated from high school. That summer
he took my place in the business, and I began to write full
time. Now, I seldom work at the studio unless Lee, who
also attends college, gets swamped. But, Mary is still very
much with us.

The day we decided to write this book, a book that would
tell the stories of people who share their lives with ghosts,
Mary seemed to know. Immediately, the activity around
the studio picked up. It was almost as if Mary was saying,
"Okay, folks, don't forget me!"

Although she seldom goes into the front of the studio
that is open to the public, the sounds of footsteps increased, barrels rolled down the hall, and lights flashed.

New phenomena occurred. For the first time, we began
to hear voices and music. The first few times, we thought
one of us had left a radio on in the next room—but of
course, we hadn't. There were other new stunts. The
sound of a bouncing ball, and the thud of a huge roll of
background paper falling to the floor were added to the
repertoire of sounds.

We have begun to talk more openly about our ghost, and
have learned that Bob's mother saw Mary several years ago
and had "neglected" to mention it. About three years before, I had told her about the ghost and she had admitted

hearing someone in high-heeled shoes pace outside her bedroom one night when we were living there. (Guess which room she was sleeping in?) Only after we began working on this book—and Bob's brother Walter told us his mother had actually seen the ghost—did she tell what really happened that night.

The footsteps had awakened her and she had slipped out of bed and peeped around the door. She saw the ghost of a woman turning the corner of the hall—a slender young woman with long brown hair in a long dress. Her description matched the one Shellie had given us years before. But at that time Shellie was so young, we thought it might have been her imagination.

We continue to work alongside Mary, and frankly, we'd miss her if she decided to leave. Do we know who Mary was and why she lives with us? No, and maybe we never will. We speculate that she was one of the young women who worked at the roadhouse. Perhaps she died in that back room. But it really doesn't matter. She's welcome to stay with us for as long as she wants. I think she knows that.

Miss Elizabeth

I'M not sure we believe in ghosts," said Carl Butler, "but there are noises and things that occur in this house we can't explain." The house is Temple Heights, a four-level antebellum Columbus mansion purchased by Carl and Dixie Butler in 1968.

From the time they moved in, the Butlers were taunted by baffling noises. The sounds of crashing pottery and shattering glassware would send them running into the next room, only to find nothing broken or even out of place. The sounds became so common that Mrs. Butler said, "Something will wake us in the night and we'll just say, 'I wonder what that was,' before going back to sleep."

The sounds of murmuring voices constantly echo throughout Temple Heights. And even though Carl Butler knows the voices are not real, he still occasionally thinks, "This time I surely left the television on,"...only to find that he didn't. Even more perplexing is hearing someone call him by *name* when no one else is in the house! Mrs. Butler hears the voices, too. "I'll think I hear Carl coming home early and think, 'I've got to go down and see who he brought with him.'"

The Butlers wondered if they indeed did have a ghost and began researching the history of Temple Heights to find a likely candidate. General Richard T. Brownrigg built the home in 1837 as a townhouse, presumably to provide his growing family with social and educational opportunities. But they lived in the house only about five years before moving back to their plantation.

Temple Heights passed through several hands before being purchased in 1887 by a retired Methodist minister, J. H. Kennebrew, and his wife. The Kennebrews had five daughters: Daisy, Laura, Jessie, Ruth, and Elizabeth. Rev. Kennebrew died and Mrs. Kennebrew's will specified that the home not be sold until all five of the daughters married. Only two daughters eventually married and by the time the last spinster daughter died in 1965, the family had been living in reduced circumstances for many years.

All of the sisters were brilliant but somewhat eccentric, and Miss Elizabeth, one of the unmarried sisters, is rumored to have been the most eccentric of all. Older residents of Columbus remember Miss Elizabeth's unusual manner of grooming. She wore chalk dust for powder, Mercurochrome for lipstick and rouge, and dyed her hair a flaming red! She was distinctive, to say the least. Her actions were as outlandish as her dress. "The Kennebrews were rather poor but did not acknowledge that," said Mr. Butler. "Miss Elizabeth would dress up in winter clothes in the summer and go up to the hotel and tell people that she was visiting in St. Petersburg (Russia) or Alaska."

After investigating the former residents of Temple Heights, the Butlers named the cause of all of the unusual phenomena occurring in their home "Miss Elizabeth." "She was very unusual," Carl Butler said; "so, we just used her name. We know a great deal about the people who have lived here and we thought she was a likely candidate to still be hanging about." They had no idea how right they were.

Even though the Butlers lived with the unusual sounds on a daily basis, they did not actually *see* anything for many years. However, some of their guests have both seen and heard things they cannot explain. Mr. Butler remembered one guest's experience: "An older lady saw a white wispy thing pass by the door to the upstairs guest room and then continue up the stairs to the top floor. Since Dixie and I aren't wispy, we assumed she saw something.

The Butlers saw the figure of a woman go through the wall in the main hallway.
Temple Heights—Entrance foyer and staircase.

She closed the door to her room, put a chair against the door, and slept with the light on." Both Butlers emphasize that this guest was an old friend they knew well and was a very intelligent, matter-of-fact person. Mrs. Butler laughed, "She did say later that she realized putting the chair against the door probably did nothing to help. But it did make her feel better."

There have been other types of phenomena the Butlers have been unable to explain. They are still wondering about a signature which simply disappeared from an upstairs bedroom door. "We knew which room was Laura Kennebrew's," Mr. Butler said, "because her name was on the door. The word 'Laura' was written on the door in pencil so heavily that it had made an impression in the wood. It had been there ever since we moved in. But when I tried to show my father the name, it had disappeared. I called Dixie and she was astounded to find, 'There's nothing here.' And we both remembered exactly where the name was and exactly how it was written. I don't know if anyone would believe that or not, but it's true. After twenty years, it just disappeared."

The Butlers believe their cats often see things they cannot. "We've always had cats, and they react as though they are seeing something we don't see," Carl Butler said. "They seem more alert than frightened. A cat asleep on the foot of our bed will suddenly sit up and watch something in the hall that we can't see."

Recently, the Butlers saw the figure of a woman go through the wall in the main hallway. The figure was too vague to identify, but during a dinner party on a hot, muggy night in July of 1991, they finally learned the identity of their unseen guest. The after-dinner conversation turned to ghosts, and a friend revealed an experience at Temple Heights that had occurred months earlier.

Temple Heights is a featured home during pilgrimage, and the Butlers' friend had been helping guide tourists through the home. During a break, she passed the Butlers' bedroom and saw the ghostly figure of a woman standing in the middle of the room. Startled, she went back downstairs, but decided to say nothing to the Butlers. Later she discussed the experience with an elderly friend. When she finished describing the apparition, her friend said, "You have just described Elizabeth Kennebrew perfectly."

The Butlers are content to share their home with Miss Elizabeth. Mr. Butler said, "We feel her presence as an ongoing thing, but it's not at all sinister. She obviously liked it here enough to hang around."

"I heard a deep voice say, 'Good morning'...and there was no one there."

An Ornament for Natchez

FREDERICK Stanton's dreams were far too big for his native Ireland. Lured by stories of great riches to be made in the American South, he left his home in Belfast in 1815. Huge fortunes in cotton were waiting in Natchez for men of ambition who were willing to work hard, and at the age of nineteen, Stanton was anxious to get his share.

Stanton shrewdly decided that a cotton broker stood to make more money than a planter—and with less risk. By the 1830s, Frederick Stanton and his wife, Hulda, were living in a Natchez mansion, Cherokee, with their growing brood of children.

With his keen business sense, Frederick Stanton had become very wealthy within a short length of time, but he had a bitter lesson to learn. During the panic of the 1830s, Frederick Stanton learned that brokers—even shrewd ones—were not immune to financial reversals. Stanton had to move his family from Cherokee to another home, Glenwood. Even though Glenwood was also a mansion, it was a step down for the Stantons.

In Stanton's mind, he had only suffered a temporary setback. Eternally optimistic, he ignored the past and forged ahead. Since he was a true workaholic, his driving ambition soon made him enormously wealthy in the boom days before the Civil War.

Stanton began to design what would be his crowning achievement, the home he boasted would be "an ornament for Natchez." He set out to build the largest and most elaborate mansion in a town known for its magnificent homes. He succeeded.

By 1857 the mansion was rising atop a hill in Natchez that covered an entire city block. After construction was underway, Stanton is believed to have left Natchez to scour Europe for furnishings to adorn his new house. If so, he returned in 1858 to a stunning sight. Surrounded by live oak trees, his home stood proudly on her hill like a queen amid her court. She was magnificent. Frederick Stanton was pleased, and named his creation "Belfast."

The Stanton family moved into their dream home in late 1858, but Frederick Stanton had little time to enjoy his mansion—he died on January 4, 1859. Soon after his death, the Civil War, which devastated the South's economy, hit the residents of Belfast (now known as Stanton Hall) as it did everyone else. After the war, Hulda Stanton struggled with the huge cost of maintaining such an enormous home. In the years following the war, most of the fine furnishings were sold.

After Mrs. Stanton's death in 1893, the home changed hands several times until 1938, when the property was acquired by the Pilgrimage Garden Club of Natchez to serve as their headquarters. They have carefully restored the old mansion, and through their efforts, Stanton Hall has been designated a National Historic Landmark.

Frederick Stanton would be pleased if he could see his magnificent home today. But according to some, he may still come by to check up on things. Mrs. Vera Daimwood, now retired as an associate manager of the Mississippi Tourism Department, never believed in the supernatural until after a visit to Stanton Hall.

"I was chaperoning Mississippi's Miss Hospitality at the Natchez Mardi Gras," she remembered. "When I took the young ladies to Natchez, we usually stayed at Stanton Hall, and at that time, a Ms. Poole was the housekeeper."

Ms. Poole had instructed Mrs. Daimwood on how to gain entrance at night to avoid tripping the elaborate alarm system. "Call me before you leave the reception so I can take the alarm system off, and you can come in the front door," she said. Once Mrs. Daimwood and Miss Hospitality were inside the mansion and in their room, which was on the second floor, Ms. Poole would reset the alarm system. Since the system worked both horizontally and vertically, they could not walk down the stairs to the first floor during the night without tripping the alarm. They were also instructed to be up and out before nine the next morning because of tour groups.

"Before we went to bed, I latched the door just in case we overslept, since we were both very tired," Mrs. Daimwood remembered. Sleep didn't come easily. "I was restless, and I heard people walking in the hall all night.

"At daybreak as the sun came up, it reflected in the armoire and woke me. I was half awake when I distinctly heard a man's voice, a very deep voice, say, 'Good morning.'" Mrs. Daimwood sat straight up in bed and looked over at her roommate but she was sleeping soundly. Shrugging, she lay back down and *again* heard a man's booming voice say, "Good morning." Puzzled, she looked around the room. All was well and the latch was still fastened. She glanced at the clock; it was six o'clock a.m. Mrs. Daimwood searched for an explanation, and finally assumed she had heard one of the yard men arriving for work.

About seven o'clock, she nudged Miss Hospitality awake and went down for breakfast. Ms. Poole was in the kitchen. "How did you rest?" she asked.

Mrs. Daimwood answered, "Fine, but your yard man really comes early."

Ms. Poole asked, "What are you talking about?"

"Well, about daybreak I heard this deep man's voice saying, 'Good morning,'" replied Mrs. Daimwood.

"But we have no men on the premises," Ms. Poole answered. "The yard people were here yesterday and they left before dark. I'd say you were fortunate."

"If I sleep in the main house, they keep me awake all night." Stanton Hall—
Porch

"I saw a shadow when I was going down the steps..." Stanton Hall—Staircase.

"But why?"

Ms. Poole smiled, "Colonel Stanton is comfortable with you. He doesn't speak to everybody."

"What on earth are you talking about?" Mrs. Daimwood asked.

Then Ms. Poole began to tell of her own experiences with the Stantons of Stanton Hall. "I've had many occasions to hear them and to speak to them," she said. "They rattle my doorknob. If I sleep in the main house, they keep me awake all night. They have even tripped the alarm system."

Mrs. Daimwood told her of the things she had heard during the night: "I heard steps all night long."

Ms. Poole replied, "You probably heard the children. When the weather was bad, the children would play in the halls."

"I also saw a shadow when I was going down the steps this morning," Mrs. Daimwood confessed. "It seemed like a little dog ran down the steps."

"What kind of dog did you see?"

"It looked like a little black Scottie or black cocker," she answered.

"They had a black cocker," Ms. Poole said. "It would run up and down the halls with the children."

Mrs. Daimwood was still not convinced she had experienced an episode of the supernatural. "I laughed it off," she said.

A few minutes later, Miss Hospitality bounced down the stairs. Ms. Poole asked the same question she had asked Mrs. Daimwood earlier, "How did you rest?"

She replied, "Fine, except for people walking in the hall all night and the man waking me up saying, 'Good morning.'"

Mrs. Daimwood and Ms. Poole looked at each other and began laughing. Mrs. Daimwood said, "I'm a believer."

"She touched my arm...it was the coldest cold I've ever felt."

Amberly's Roommate

WHEN Nancy Reeves' apartment was flooded in 1987, she had no time to make a leisurely search for new housing. She quickly found a small two-bedroom house in Petal and moved in with her daughter, Amberly. The house was old and drafty, but initially she didn't sense anything strange.

"As soon as we moved in," Ms. Reeves said, "Amberly started mentioning that she saw someone in her room. She didn't want to go into her bedroom at night. But since she was only six or seven years old, I thought it was just childish imagination, and I downplayed it. I'd go open the closet door and say, 'See, there's nothing in there.'"

But, one hot July night five months later, Ms. Reeves came face to face with an apparition that frightened her so badly she moved the very next day.

"I was lying in bed reading a book; it was a juicy romance and I was wide awake. For some reason, I looked up and *I saw a figure coming down the hall.* It seemed to be a young woman with long hair. She was a bluish-white color and not transparent at all even though her features weren't distinct." As the figure grew closer, Ms. Reeves literally froze! "There was no getting up, no screaming. I just couldn't do anything, but I was thinking, 'This is not real.' It seemed like it took her forever to walk from the hall to my bed, but it was really a very short space, because the room was so tiny. She glided to the side of the bed, reached an arm out, and touched my arm with her hand. It was the coldest cold I've ever felt, a cold that went all the way to the bone."

The figure turned and began to move toward the hall in the direction of Amberly's room. At that point, Ms. Reeves' paralysis broke. She jumped out of bed and ran toward the figure screaming, "No! You can't go in there!" When it got to the middle of the hall, it disappeared. Ms. Reeves raced into Amberly's room and scooped her up in her arms. "I'm a Baptist, but I had a rosary given to me by a dear friend. I put it around Amberly's neck and put her in the bed with me. I don't know why I thought I could have saved her from anything, but the only thing I could think was, 'If I ever get out of here, I'll never come back.'" Even though there was time remaining on the lease, Ms. Reeves and Amberly moved the next day.

A neighbor asked Ms. Reeves why she was moving, and when she hesitated he said, "I can tell you why. You *saw* something." That's when she learned that other occupants of the small house had moved abruptly—after being frightened by something they couldn't explain!

"The stereo was unplugged, but it was still playing!"

Hilltop

ILLTOP, a property consisting of two large old homes and several outbuildings, lies in old Enterprise. The homes sit atop an ancient hill, guarded by colossal oak trees that were full-grown before the time of the Civil War.

The older home, the Lee-Mitts house, was built in 1830 by a Dr. Lee and is known as the "Colonial" house. During the Civil War, a small church next to the property was converted into a Confederate hospital and the overflow of wounded soldiers was housed in Dr. Lee's home.

In the late 1800s, Dr. Lee's widow sold the home to the Swan family, who had moved to Enterprise from Minnesota to take advantage of the booming timber industry. After the Swan family left, the home was purchased by a Mr. Parker.

The other home, a traditional Queen Anne Victorian, was built by the Swans on the site of an old cabin. It is simply called the "Victorian" house and was purchased by the Mitts family when one of the Swan brothers went back to Minnesota. Ms. Chandler Mitts, whose family now owns the entire complex, is convinced both houses are haunted. Few people who have spent any time in either of the houses would disagree.

Ms. Mitts' father was born in the Victorian home and as a boy was friends with Mr. Parker, the owner of the Colonial house. Mr. Parker cherished his home and told his sons, "If you ever sell my home, *I'll come back and haunt you.*" After Mr. Parker's death, the sons sold his home and the house began to get a reputation for being haunted.

"Three families that I know of have moved out of that house," said Chandler Mitts. "One moved out after the third night saying it was haunted. Till this day, the woman refuses to come in the house."

Ms. Mitts' father bought Mr. Parker's home and moved in with his family in 1955. "This was a spooky house for a kid," Ms. Mitts said. "There were always *sounds* through-out the house. The chandeliers move and sparkle and make sounds for no reason at all. The piano strikes single notes—almost like a cat is hitting the keys. The sounds in the walls are indescribable—a rhythmic noise. And the doors shut by themselves. You can hear voices but you can't understand them. Pictures move for no reason and the lights turn on and off by themselves.

"Whenever my sisters and my brother and I would get frightened, Daddy would just say, 'Well, Mr. Parker, come on in.' He just passed it off that way.

"Daddy told us that Mr. Parker liked us and he was a friend and didn't mind us living in his house. We were afraid, but we weren't *really* afraid because we believed what Daddy said.

"I see images pass through the kitchen, the living room, and the dining room," Ms. Mitts said. "I always have to check them out. It's like seeing a movie and you know something is in the room, and you say to the person in the movie, 'Don't go in there, you fool! Why is she going in there?' But you've got to go or you go out of your mind.

"Other people swear that the only reason we can live in the house is that Mr. Parker handpicked us," Ms. Mitts said.

For Ms. Mitts, unusual dreams are a part of the phenom-ena at the Colonial house. "I have had a recurring dream since I was eight years old," she said. "It's a dream of a photograph of five people. There is a man with a beard and his wife, mother-in-law, a daughter, and one additional person. They all look very stern, almost a Quaker look. The mother-in-law has gray hair and she is wearing a black dress with a high collar. I can't explain why I keep having the same dream.

"I have heard that elegant parties took place many years ago in this house. The parlor and dining room would be combined for ballroom dancing. And as a child, I had a very strange dream about dancing in this house that I've never forgotten," Chandler Mitts said.

"I never took dancing as a child. I ran away from home once because my mother wanted me to take ballet lessons, and I was such a tomboy that I didn't want to. But one night, I dreamed that I danced all night. I couldn't believe I was dancing so well. The piano was playing and the chandeliers were swaying. I was turning and leaping, and I danced and danced through the dining room and living room. When I awoke the next morning, every muscle in my body was sore. I could barely move."

The Victorian house, which has been home to the Mitts family for almost a century, has its share of strange happenings as well. The house was almost destroyed in February of 1990 when a tornado sent a huge oak tree through its roof. Chandler Mitts was advised that the house was damaged beyond repair. But she was determined to rebuild the house and credits her ancestors for showing her how to do the impossible. "I went up in the attic about three in the morning. I called on anything I had ever loved and lost. How could I save the house? Then it hit me. I knew exactly what to do and how to do it."

Ms. Mitts undertook the massive rebuilding, determined not only to save the house, but to use parts of the centuries-old oak trees that had also fallen victim to the high winds. "They were majestic trees," she said. "One of the trees was forty-eight inches in diameter. We had played around it as kids, and Confederate soldiers had sat under it during the Civil War while waiting to be seen by Dr. Lee. A lot of the house has been rebuilt with wood from those huge oak trees."

As the rebuilding progressed, work crews began to complain. "Workers would come running out of the house saying they were never going back inside," Ms. Mitts remembered. "The stereo, which was on the second floor, kept coming on and frightening them. We even unplugged it, but as soon as the work crew would go back into the gables on the third floor, it would start playing. One guy said, 'I don't care if I lose my job, that stereo is still on.' I checked. The stereo was unplugged, but it was still playing!

"The head of the work crew laughed himself silly at his workers, until one day when he was working around the electrical panel," Ms. Mitts said. "He *knew* that someone was standing at the top of the servants' stairs looking at him. He glanced up, but no one was there. He went back to work, and, once again, he knew someone was staring at him. When he looked up, they had disappeared again. He turned and almost bumped into someone. He automatically said, 'Excuse me,' but no one was there. He knew then that what his men had been saying was true."

Doors slam and open windows fall shut for no apparent reason in the Victorian house. Sounds of walking up and down the halls are common along with the sounds of falling objects. "I'll think something fell off a table and broke or cracked, but when I go in the room, I don't see anything," Ms. Mitts said.

The Mitts' dogs are aware of unseen presences. "Feather will not go into the Victorian house at night," Ms. Mitts said. "She'll stare at the top of the servants' stairs and I can call her and she'll ignore me. She'll continue to stare at the top of those stairs like she's seeing something. She'll run into the hall like she sees something and then just stand there and wag her tail. My sister's dog will stand on the servants' stairs and stare at something that isn't there. And the dogs go berserk in the Colonial house.

"This entire hill is engulfed by presences," said Chandler Mitts. "A lot of it is the Confederate soldiers. When those beautiful old oak trees fell, it was the 125th anniversary of when the Confederate soldiers sat under them. I said, 'It's those damn Yankees come back to haunt us.'"

But she laughed as she recalled how the Yankees got blamed for stealing the Lee family silver. "The family cursed the Yankees because they stole the family silver. Many years after the war, the children were chasing each other around an old gooseneck rocker and knocked off the back of it. The missing family silver tumbled out! They had blamed the Yankees all of those years."

Chandler Mitts recalled an incident that happened late one night. "I heard a hammering sound in the barn. It was the sound of driving nails. I was afraid I was being robbed so I went down to check it out. Halfway there, the hammering stopped. I turned to go back to the house and the hammering started again. It was the unmistakable sound of driving nails. Well, you don't have to slap *me* in the face. I knew what it was."

The Mitts family has experienced many tragedies at Hilltop which could account for some of the hauntings. The tragedies include a great-grandfather who was kicked and killed by a pony, a grandmother who fell down the steps in the Victorian house and lost the twins she was carrying, and a horseman who was killed in an accident.

Ms. Mitts doesn't feel threatened by the unseen spirits she shares Hilltop with. "I believe you can be reached by presences if you can be trusted—and if you don't make light of them and joke about them. It's a trust factor, like so much else in life."

"One night we heard a crying-out coming from the upstairs...."

Refuge for a Genius

ALTHOUGH Rowan Oak was built around 1844 by Colonel Robert Sheegog, it will forever be known as the home of literary lion William Faulkner. When Faulkner moved into the two-story white structure in 1930, it was one of hundreds of deteriorating relics of pre-Civil War days still standing throughout the South. Rowan Oak, like similar old homes with owners who had fallen on hard times, lacked such niceties as electricity and indoor plumbing. Working alongside the carpenters and painters, Faulkner helped paint, hang wallpaper, and install pipes. As a final mark of ownership, he renamed the house "Rowan Oak" after the Scottish legend of the rowan tree:

"Rawn-tree in red-threed

Pits the witches t' their speed."

Faulkner, haunted by demons from within and without, expected Rowan Oak to hold the line at least against the evil spirits from without. It became his refuge, an oasis of peace and quiet in his troubled world. As visitors pass through the gate, quiet and solitude strike suddenly; the only sounds are those of birds and crickets singing in the stately cedar and magnolia trees. Just steps from a thriving Oxford neighborhood, Rowan Oak is a remote, rural world unto itself. A double row of ancient cedars lines the brick walkway leading to the front door. Once visitors step over the threshold, they are in the world of William Faulkner. Visitors move quietly through the rooms, feeling like intruders into a very private past. The feeling is not that of a carefully maintained museum; it is as if the

Faulkners are merely out for the afternoon. Howard Bahr is curator of the museum, which is owned and maintained by the University of Mississippi. He holds both the home and the man who lived there in awe. "I love this old house," he said with sincerity.

But few people want to be alone inside Rowan Oak after dark, including Howard Bahr. The atmosphere of the old house, which hangs heavy even during daylight hours, descends at night like a suffocating cloak. "It's terrifying here at night," he said. Do ghosts roam the halls of Rowan Oak? Apparently so.

William Faulkner himself told ghost stories about his home. His most popular tale was the tragic story of Judith Sheegog, daughter of the builder of Rowan Oak. In Faulkner's story, Judith had done the unthinkable—she had fallen in love with a Yankee soldier. Certain her father would never approve of the match, she and her lover decided to elope. Late one night, Judith hung a rope ladder outside her bedroom window and began to climb down. Her anxious lover watched in horror as she slipped and fell to her death by hitting her head on the brick sidewalk.

Faulkner seemed convinced Judith's ghost haunted the old mansion. He said he had seen the ghost, and both he and his wife claimed to have heard footsteps and piano music coming from the parlor. There is only one thing wrong with this traditional Southern ghost story of lost love: according to Howard Bahr, Judith Sheegog never existed.

"There was no Judith Sheegog," he said. "In the Sheegog genealogy, there is no one named Judith." Bahr has his own idea why Faulkner invented Judith's tragic story. "I think Mr. Faulkner made up the story to explain away some of the noises he heard in this old house," he said.

"We hear sounds like walking," Mr. Bahr said. "And sometimes I hear things falling, and when I go into the room the sound came from, everything is fine."

He has also heard the sound of a man's laughter followed

w people want to be alone inside Rowan Oak after dark.   Rowan Oak—Front view.

"Sometimes I hear things falling, and when I go into the room the sound came from, everything is fine." Rowan Oak—Wall in Faulkner's study.

by footsteps which seemed to pass close to him. But he emphasized, "No one here has actually *seen* anything."

Mr. Bahr had rather not be at Rowan Oak after dark, but when it is necessary, he makes sure he has companions. Even so, the sounds continue. "One night we heard a crying-out coming from the upstairs," he remembered. "It sounded like an old person crying out. It was upsetting."

Mr. Bahr had an explanation for the strange happenings at Rowan Oak: "These old houses have so much life in them that something is bound to leak out from time to time."

*He awoke in the middle
of the night to see a girl
looking down at him.*

The House Party at
Twelve Oaks

JOE and Kay Adams of Jackson never believed in ghosts
until they moved to Twelve Oaks, their Gautier vaca-
tion home. The lovely old home, built around 1869 on
the site of an antebellum hotel, appears peaceful and tran-
quil with its broad porches caressed by gentle gulf breezes
—hardly the setting for a menagerie of ghosts. But one
night, soon after Hurricane Elena, the Adamses realized
they had permanent guests.

"We were down checking on the new roof that was being
put on. The children weren't with us," Mrs. Adams remembered. "Joe and I sleep in the front bedroom by the end of
the stairs and the children sleep upstairs. About two
o'clock a.m. our dog started to growl. We awoke and
looked toward the stairs to see which child was coming
down—we forgot the children weren't with us. I saw a man
going up the steps. The first thing I thought was that we
had a burglar."

It never occurred to Mrs. Adams that the intruder was
anything other than the flesh and blood variety. "We
reached for the telephone beside the bed and called the
sheriff. They were there in two minutes. They searched the
house, but, of course, they found nothing. I felt like an
idiot, but they were really nice. We had a cup of coffee, and
then they checked the house one more time...attics...every-
thing. We went back to bed, but about an hour and a half
later, we heard a voice out in the hallway saying 'ooooooh.'

Joe sat straight up in bed, and we just looked at each other. Neither of us could bring ourselves to get up and go look."

Mrs. Adams mentioned her experience with the male ghost to their caretaker and asked if he had ever seen anything unusual around the house. He looked at her in amazement and replied, "This is for real, isn't it, Mrs. Adams?" When she answered "yes," the Adamses found they had yet another ghost in residence.

"I've been scared to tell you this," the caretaker confessed, "but there's this little old lady who watches me out of the den window. Sometimes she's standing and sometimes she's rocking. I see her all the time. I can be working in the yard and see her and then turn or look down and when I look back up, she'll be gone. But I see her all the time." He described the woman in detail—down to her stooped shoulders and white curls. Later the Adamses discovered this description matched that of the mother of the man they bought the house from! In her later years, she loved to sit at the window and watch the activity surrounding the house.

A couple of years later, the Adamses became aware of still *another* ghost, that of a young girl. "When our daughter, Linden, had nightmares, she would come and get in the bed with us," Mrs. Adams explained. "One night when Linden was about ten, we thought we heard her coming down the steps. We looked up and saw a figure coming down the stairs with long blonde hair and wearing a long white nightgown—just like Linden. There is a point at the bottom of the steps when you lose sight because of the way the door of the bedroom is positioned, and we kept waiting for Linden to come in the room. She never did. So finally, Joe got up to look for her and found her in her bed, fast asleep."

The Adamses have seen the little girl several times. And houseguests have heard her talking as if she is talking to a pet or a doll, but only the Adamses have actually seen her.

"We looked up and saw a figure coming down the stairs with long blond hair and wearing a long white nightgown." Twelve Oaks—Staircase.

The Adamses have tried to identify the spirits that share their home. Other than the old woman, they have been able to positively identify only one of their permanent guests, the spirit of a teenage girl. The Adamses have not been privileged to see her, but a houseguest spent a rather uneasy night due to her presence.

A male visitor was spending the night in the Adamses' front bedroom. He awoke in the middle of the night to see a girl looking down at him. He described her in detail— very dark hair in a 1920s bob style with bangs, a part in the middle, and curls around the ears. He closed his eyes and then opened them. *The girl was still there.*

Mrs. Adams laughed, "He couldn't move, but he didn't know if he actually was not able to move or if he was just so scared he couldn't move. He said the only thing he could do at that point was to hope for the best and go back to sleep." The next time he opened his eyes, she was gone. His description of the girl was so detailed that a neighbor recognized it as her sister. She produced a photograph of her sister... he identified the girl as his unearthly visitor.

According to her sister, the woman had lived to a ripe old age. Why would her ghost appear as a young woman? Mrs. Adams may have the answer: "She was supposed to have been the happiest when she was at Twelve Oaks. Maybe ghosts come to places where they were happy."

Perhaps the spirits of the man and small girl remain from the antebellum hotel, but Mrs. Adams has wondered if the man is Henry Gautier, the builder of the house. "It's just speculation, but he would have had a strong attachment for his home. The ghost was about the right size to have been Gautier and was wearing a white shirt and light trousers. Henry Gautier was known for wearing white suits." Adding to the evidence the ghost could be Gautier is the fact that he has been seen upstairs carrying a lantern and disappearing through a closet door which leads to a secret room. Who better than the builder of a home to know all of its secrets? Regardless of their visitors' identities, the

Adamses are used to sharing their home with their unseen guests. "The ghosts don't disturb anything," Kay Adams mused. "They seem perfectly content with what they do— which is just to wander around." And why not? The Adamses have carefully restored and meticulously maintained the home the former inhabitants must have loved.

"Suddenly, hot water began flowing out of a dead pipe."

King's Tavern

THE origins of King's Tavern are lost in the mists of history, but some historians believe it was built as early as the 1760s. Standing at the southern end of the Natchez Trace, King's Tavern was an oasis for weary travelers and a gathering place for the early citizens of Natchez. The three-story building, built from brick, cypress, and boat timbers, resembles an ancient fortress with its barred windows and block-like construction. And for many years, it did in fact serve as a bulwark against the surrounding wilderness.

Richard King became owner of the building in 1789 and operated a tavern on the premises. According to legend, he had a mistress named Madeline who worked as a serving girl. During those years, much of the early history of the Natchez area revolved around the old tavern. Through its doors came the generations of pioneers and politicians and murderers and millionaires who would people the pages of American history.

The first United States mail to the region was carried down the Natchez Trace by Indian runners and brought to King's Tavern. A small room on the first floor served as the post office. Aaron Burr and his cohorts plotted their grand schemes in the tavern's low-ceilinged rooms, and Andrew Jackson visited during the years he lived in the area.

The tavern was always a boisterous and exciting—if dangerous—place. Bullet holes are still embedded in the heavy doors, and the imprints of both bear and cougar paws are visible in the floor. Perhaps the excitement was just too much for the inhabitants of King's Tavern to leave, even after their deaths. Generations of both owners and visitors have sworn the tavern is haunted, and few people who have spent any time in the old building disagree.

Today, King's Tavern is a restaurant where supernatural happenings are common. "Literally hundreds of people have had experiences in here," said Yvonne Scott, owner/ manager of the tavern. The prime suspect of the phenomena is Madeline, Richard King's mistress, and most new employees get a swift introduction to her pranks.

"The first night I worked here," Stephanie Burts said, "I was sitting at one of the tables eating and I heard a ball bounce and someone walking upstairs. Everything upstairs had already been turned off and locked up."

Another employee, Sonjia Frost, said, "One night Stephanie and I took the garbage out. We had turned off the lights upstairs, but when we got outside, all of the upstairs lights were blazing. When we went back inside, they were off. But from the outside, they looked like they were on. Also at certain times of night, the lights will dim at the bar. And we hear footsteps *all* of the time.

"Madeline likes water," Ms. Frost continued. "One night a puddle of water just appeared on the floor. People have told me that they'll be on the second floor and water will start dripping on their heads. They'll move and it'll start dripping on their heads again in a different place.

"The water also turns off and on by itself behind the bar," Ms. Frost said. "I've seen it. I've reached over to turn the taps off and they were already off. I've felt the pipes and they *feel* hot but there is no hot water line into those particular pipes. The water coming out of all of the other pipes will be cold."

Why does Madeline "have a thing" about water? "I have no earthly idea," laughed Ms. Scott, "unless it's warm where she is!"

Ms. Scott has had her own problems with the plumbing system at the tavern. "There was no hot water upstairs

In the 1930s, three skeletons were unearthed in the tavern. King's Tavern.

when we first opened. One day I was in the bathroom upstairs discussing plumbing repairs, and I reached over and turned on the faucet even though I knew the pipes weren't hooked up. Suddenly, hot water began flowing out of a dead pipe. The man who was with me said I left high heel marks on his back getting out of that bathroom!"

Madeline is also blamed when the alarms go off at five o'clock and six o'clock in the mornings. Many times the police have been summoned, only to find no evidence of any intruder, except for one inside door open on the second floor. It is always the same door, and a door that could not be reached unless the outside doors and windows had been tampered with.

Madeline enjoys playing with the waitress station door. "It is very heavy," Ms. Frost said, "and it will stop in mid-swing like someone is holding it. It will stand still for a while, then swing shut."

"The swinging door has happened to me twice," said Yvonne Scott. "I just said, 'O.K. Madeline, let it go,' and both times, she did. I've also felt a touch on my shoulder. I know that someone has touched me, but of course, no one is there."

In the past, workers have found small footprints in an upstairs bathroom. The footsteps seemed to start as if someone had climbed out of the bathtub with wet feet and stepped onto the floor. The footsteps abruptly ended at the door. Since a spider web remained intact in the tub, it did not appear water could have been turned on anytime recently.

Ms. Scott told of a friend's experience which seems to indicate that Madeline still intends to keep her customers happy. "There is a dumbwaiter that goes to the second floor," Ms. Scott said. "One night a man came in late and ordered wine. The wine is kept upstairs and the person with the key to the liquor storeroom had already locked up and gone home. They apologized to the customer but told him there was no way they could get the wine since they didn't have a key. Then they heard the dumbwaiter come down and when they opened it, the bottle of wine he ordered was sitting on it!"

Madeline seems to consider the attic her private domain. "She doesn't like for people to go into the attic," one employee said. "She gets upset and blows lights. One night she blew every light on the second floor."

Several people have seen Madeline's ghost, but hers is not the only spirit seen. The ghost of an Indian in full war bonnet has been spotted by employees in the part of the building that used to be the post office. One day a little girl saw a man in the mirror at the bar. She asked her mother who the man with the funny red hat was. Her mother answered, "There is no man with a red hat." The girl insisted, "Yes, there is," and pointed at the mirror adding, "and Mommy, he's not nice." Employees wonder if she saw the ghost of one of the Indians who ran the mail up and down the trace.

Perhaps the most upsetting phenomenon that occurs on a regular basis is the sound of a baby crying. "One day I was putting crackers on the tables and I heard a baby crying," Ms. Frost said. "I looked everywhere. I thought that maybe someone was applying for a job and brought a baby with them. But the cook and I were the only ones in the building. Even though I didn't think the noise could be coming from the street since the building's thick walls make it almost soundproof, I went outside and looked, but no one was there. The crying sounds as though it is coming from the wall in the old post room or the dumbwaiter on the other side of the wall."

Yvonne Scott has also heard the crying baby. "One day, I was sitting at my desk in the kitchen and I heard a baby crying," she said. She turned to the cook and a waitress who were in the room with her and asked, "What was that?" The waitress answered, "That was a baby," and ran to the front to check. The three women were alone in the building.

Ms. Scott has noticed a connection between the frequency of trips to the attic and the crying baby. "Every time we go into the attic, we hear the baby cry within a day or two," she said. "When I heard the crying sound, we had been in the attic the day before."

Sonjia Frost told a horrifying story that has been passed down for generations that may explain the ghostly baby: "One day a mother and her baby were in the mailroom. The baby began crying and the mother was trying to comfort it. The outlaw Big Harpe was in the tavern in the adjoining room. He went into the mailroom with what the mother thought was the intention of helping quiet the baby. Instead, he picked up the infant by its ankles and slammed it against the wall, killing it."

Crying babies and Indians aside, Madeline seems to be the predominant spirit at King's Tavern. She seems determined, not only to be remembered, but to sample some of the cosmetics of twentieth-century women. Even customers have fallen prey to her experiments. One woman had an especially unnerving adventure.

"She came out of the restroom very upset," Sonjia Frost said. "She had outlined her lips with lipstick, but the color didn't follow the lines of her lips—there was a smeared red outline well outside her lips making her look like a clown. She said she had been putting on her lipstick, but when she looked in the mirror, the line was outside her lips. She tried to scrub the lipstick off and then looked back into the mirror to try again. She saw an image looking back at her that was not her own. It was the face of a young woman with reddish hair. She had been putting lipstick on the larger lips of the woman in the mirror."

A picture of a young woman hangs on the wall of the downstairs women's restroom. Ms. Scott found the picture by accident—or so she thought at the time:

"I was on my way to work one morning and passed a flea market that had been there for years," she remembered. "I decided to stop because I'm always looking for things to put on the walls here. I walked into the back room and a picture caught my eye. It was just what I thought Madeline would look like. I picked up the picture and took it up front and the lady said, 'Where did you get this?' I said, 'In the back room.' She replied, 'I've been working here a year and a half and I've never seen this picture.'

   "I put it in the ladies' restroom. It's a picture of a very pretty young woman, very seductive, with an impish look. She's holding an apple and wearing a low-cut period dress. I think it must look a lot like Madeline."

   In the 1930s, three skeletons were unearthed in the tavern. Two belonged to men. One belonged to a young woman of sixteen or seventeen. A jeweled dagger was found close by. Could Madeline have met an untimely death along with two unfortunate companions? No one will ever likely know. But Madeline is welcome to stay at King's Tavern. "She's not vengeful," Ms. Scott said. "She's just mischievous and wants us to know she's here. Madeline keeps us on our toes."

"I didn't believe in ghosts before I came here.... They have made a believer out of me."

Vicksburg's Cedar Grove

CEDAR Grove, built in the 1840s by John Klein atop a bluff overlooking the Mississippi River, has had a rich and checkered history during its one hundred and fifty years. One of the largest antebellum mansions in the entire South, it has been silent witness to a parade of historical characters seldom matched in Mississippi history.

Before the war, Cedar Grove was the site of elegant balls attended by Southern notables such as Jefferson Davis. But much to Vicksburg's horror, Klein's wife Elizabeth, who was a native of Ohio, was a relative of the hated Union general, William Tecumseh Sherman. Sherman also danced across the shining floors of Cedar Grove's ballroom.

The first shots fired at Vicksburg during the Civil War went through the doors and floors of the huge mansion. In fact, a cannonball still lies embedded in the parlor wall, and a jagged hole remains in the parlor floor from that bombardment. Soon after the shelling started, however, General Sherman assured the Kleins their home would be spared, and he personally escorted the family to safety. Sherman and the Union Army took over the house, and Union forces remained there until after the fall of Vicksburg.

According to legend, Union General Ulysses S. Grant slept in the enormous four-poster bed in the master bedroom following Vicksburg's surrender. When the Kleins moved back into their home a few months later, Union soldiers still occupied the first floor.

Elizabeth Klein, her family, and her magnificent home survived the war, but she would pay a harsh penalty for the rest of her life: she would always be considered an outcast by the citizens of Vicksburg. Not even the accidental shooting on the back stairs of her son, Willie (named after the despised general), would thaw the hearts of Vicksburg. Townspeople said sixteen-year-old Willie's death was due to the curse Elizabeth had placed on him by naming him after Sherman.

Today, Cedar Grove is beautifully preserved as a monument to those halcyon days before the war. Huge Tuscan columns support wide galleries on both the front and rear of the mansion. Inside, marble mantels, exquisite plaster work, crystal chandeliers, and original furnishings make it seem as if the Kleins have never left. And perhaps they haven't.

Peggy Shaeffer, manager at Cedar Grove, has witnessed many things she cannot explain. "Mr. Klein used to sit in the gentlemen's parlor each night and smoke his pipe before he retired," she said. "Even though we haven't allowed smoking in the house for some time now, we often smell a strong tobacco scent in the room late in the afternoon. The odor is very distinct. I have smelled it and so have hostesses, the owners, and guests. It doesn't happen every day, but it's fairly frequent."

Ms. Shaeffer also wonders if Mr. Klein declares his presence in another way. Next to the cabinet in the gentlemen's parlor which holds Mr. Klein's favorite meerschaum pipe, sits a small table. On it is displayed a photograph of the present owners. "Often I'll walk into the room and the photograph is turned face down. I'll set it up, and later on I'll check and it'll be turned back down."

Perhaps the most unsettling sound that recurs at Cedar Grove is the sound of children playing and a baby crying. "Elizabeth had ten children, but only six lived to be adults," Ms. Shaeffer said. "We know that two children died in the nursery. The Klein's first child was a daughter who died when she was two. They also had a boy who died at two months. I've heard the sound of a baby crying in the nursery several times. It sounds like an infant. I can also hear children walking, running, and scurrying around in the nursery area."

According to Ms. Shaeffer, one of the home's later owners was a doctor whose sister committed suicide in the ballroom by shooting herself. "No one ever knew why. She was a beautiful woman," Ms. Shaeffer said. "But in the years since her death, several people have heard a gunshot and the sound of glass shattering in the ballroom." When people run toward the sound, nothing is ever found.

"I've never actually seen anything," she continued, "but I've heard things. Often when I'm here by myself in the wintertime, when it's slow and the house is locked, I hear someone walking on the second floor and hear doors slamming. I've gone up to check and could find nothing."

Others, though, have claimed to see shadowy figures. "One of the hosts saw a shadow coming down the stairs," she said. "And the stairs were creaking when he saw the shadow."

According to Ms. Shaeffer, a former manager saw a woman dressed in an antebellum gown walk down the front stairs and disappear. "He left out the nearest door very quickly," she laughed. "He recognized the woman. Before her death, she was a tour guide here. She always laughed and said, 'When I die, I'm going to come right back and stay here at Cedar Grove.' He said she was wearing the dress she always wore for pilgrimage. The dress is still stored in the basement.

"More experiences occur at night," she continued. "We've heard someone walking across the gallery at night. One night I heard someone scream, and then I heard a sound like someone falling down the stairs. I thought that one of the workers was playing a trick on me, but he wasn't even in the house. He was outside closing shutters. Another time I felt something had just rushed by me. Even the

"I've heard people running—actually running—down the stairs." Cedar
Grove—Staircase

flowers on the table were moving but nothing was there.

"We hear crashing noises all the time, especially from the basement. They sound like something is broken but nothing ever is," she said.

In fact, the basement is the source of another mystery. In the 1960s the house mysteriously caught on fire. The fire went straight across the basement of the house along a single beam. The beam is charred—not merely singed—but the surrounding wood is unharmed. The cause of the fire was never discovered.

The house has changed hands several times over the past few decades. "One family," Ms. Shaeffer said, "couldn't take all of the noises and episodes with the ghosts. It was too much of an experience for them to go through." Even though the unseen guests at Cedar Grove may have been frightening to some, Ms. Shaeffer and the other workers take them in stride. "I've never been afraid here," she said.

"I didn't believe in ghosts before I came here. But I have no explanation for the things I have heard. I have no explanation for the walking when no one is there...the doors slamming. I've heard people running—actually running—down the stairs. They have made a believer out of me."

*" I saw Dr. Nutt standing under
a tree...and I just don't need
to be here anymore!"*

Haller Nutt's Unfinished Masterpiece

*L*ONGWOOD can easily be called the most unusual
antebellum mansion in the South. Without question, it
is the largest octagonal home in the United States. Its
oriental style, with Moorish arches and massive onion-
shaped dome, manifests its splendor in haughty isolation
on the outskirts of Natchez amid a park-like expanse of
trees and shrubs.

Dr. Haller Nutt, who was a planter, scientist, and inven-
tor, wanted his home to stand in sharp contrast to the
Greek Revival mansions most Natchez citizens were building in the mid-1800s. Longwood was to be a palace which
would rise to six levels and contain thirty-two rooms. It
was to be home to Dr. Nutt, his wife Julia, and their many
children, and no expense was spared either in the building
of the home or in the ordering of rare and expensive furnishings to fill its rooms.

Construction began in 1860 and progressed with amazing speed. By early 1861, the exterior was completed,
except for some final touches, and the basement was finished. Then the Civil War began and all of the northern
craftsmen Dr. Nutt had hired returned to their homes.
Nutt, Julia, and their children moved into the basement
and waited for the war to end.

The war ruined Nutt. Although he was an ardent Union
supporter, his plantations in Louisiana (which were the

basis of his wealth) were destroyed by Union soldiers. He died in 1864, a devastated and dejected man who had helplessly paced the unfinished floors of his castle, powerless to change fate.

Julia lived on in the basement with her children, and fought to feed and clothe them in the aftermath of the Civil War. Eventually, she brought a successful lawsuit against the United States for destroying the property of a known Union sympathizer, but her settlement was not enough to finish her husband's dream. Their mansion became known around Natchez as "Nutt's Folly."

Today Longwood is the property of the Pilgrimage Garden Club of Natchez and is a National Historic Landmark. Dr. Nutt's fairy-tale home is preserved down to the hammers and chisels left lying in the upper floors by the departing workmen. Visitors wander through the oddly shaped rooms of the basement area and gaze up through the unfinished floors in awe to experience the magnificence of Haller Nutt's unfinished masterpiece. Tour guides enthrall them with the story of Longwood—perhaps with a little prompting from the Nutts themselves.

Sandra Frank, a former tour guide at Longwood, had several strange experiences while she was giving tours. "When the tour would get to the master bedroom, I would give a lot of statistics, including how many slaves and how much land Dr. Nutt owned. Sometimes I would say those statistics so many times in a day that I would get the numbers mixed up. If I got anything wrong, the lights would blink. If I tried *deliberately* making a mistake, the lights wouldn't blink, but every time I made an unconscious error they would blink. It was strange, and I never got accustomed to it.

"I had a tourist leave on me one day," she laughed. "I had accidentally made a mistake and the lights blinked. The man asked, 'What caused *that*?' I answered, 'The lights just blinked.' He observed, 'They didn't blink in any of the other rooms.' Then I said, 'Oh, it's just Dr. Nutt reminding

"I put out my cigarette and started walking into the house when I passed by an area that smelled like a very sweet perfume."
Longwood—Front view.

"When the tour would get to the master bedroom, I would give a lot of statistics... If got anything wrong, the lights would blink." Longwood—Dr. Nutt's bedroom.

me I made a mistake.' He looked at his wife and said while backing out of the room, 'I think I'll wait for you outside.'"

Mrs. Louise Burns, the resident hostess at Longwood, had a memorable encounter with an unseen presence. Her head was lifted off her pillow, then very gently laid back down. She surmises that if she was being inspected, she must have passed muster since she has been at Longwood for over twenty years.

Members of Mrs. Burns' family, maids, tour guides, and garden workers have all encountered the Nutts through the years. One of Mrs. Burns' grandsons once spotted Nutt sitting in a chair in her room. Another grandson sighted Julia, who seems to have a penchant for appearing on the stairs.

One morning a maid was dusting in the stairway room. As she scanned the room, she saw a lady standing on the stairs in a pink hoopskirt. As she tried to see her face, the figure vanished. The maid was convinced she had seen Julia. The maid, who announced she "wasn't afraid of the Devil itself," stayed. Not all the help has felt the same way:

One morning the grounds keeper came out of the garage riding the tractor. He saw Dr. Nutt standing under the tree, wearing knee breeches and "fluff"—possibly a large bow tie—around his neck. The grounds keeper rode the tractor back into the garage...and left! He returned on payday, wife in tow, to collect his paycheck. Mrs. Burns, who had assumed he was sick or hurt, asked him what had happened. He said, "I saw Dr. Nutt standing under a tree...and I just don't need to be here anymore!"

Many members of the staff have had unusual experiences. Grace Roberts remembers one day when she was standing outside, smoking. "There was no breeze and nothing blooming," she remembered. "I put out my cigarette and started walking into the house when I passed by an area that smelled like a very sweet perfume." Puzzled, she walked into the gift shop and told Mrs. Burns, who replied, "You probably walked by an area where Julia was standing."

Blinking lights, footsteps on stairs, and the sounds of children playing have all been reported at Longwood. But they seldom seem to bother the thousands of tourists who come each year to enjoy Haller Nutt's dream. The tour guides continue to give accurate information on Longwood and her builder to each and every visitor—Dr. Nutt personally sees to that.

The Boy in the Yellow Shirt

VINCENT Rog never believed in ghosts, never paid the slightest attention to the fantasies of others...at least not until he came face to face with the boy in the yellow shirt. His story began, though, with a tale told to him by his cousin.

On the way to work one morning, Mr. Rog's cousin was driving down Big Ridge Road in the Biloxi/Ocean Springs area. Suddenly, he noticed a teenage boy standing by the side of the road. The boy was wearing a yellow shirt and looking at the ground. His actions were strange enough for Rog's cousin to wonder if something was wrong. Concerned, he stopped his car and backed up, but the boy had vanished. Baffled, he drove on, and minutes later, he rounded a bad curve and was almost hit head-on by a truck. When he told his friends about the puzzling incident later at work he was surprised to hear one of his fellow workers reply, "I've seen that boy before. Something like that happened to me." The worker then related a story of seeing a boy in a yellow shirt on Big Ridge Road shortly before barely avoiding a bad accident.

Rog patiently listened to his cousin's story. "He was serious, and he believed the boy was the ghost of a teenager who was killed around that curve." Rog wasn't convinced; "I blew it off." Ghosts weren't his thing...then.

Months later Rog was riding down Big Ridge Road with

his good friend, Joe. The two young men had been partying and were in high spirits. "We were coming up on that same curve and I saw someone standing by the road in a yellow shirt so I slowed down. I didn't think anything about it until later. We weren't going fast, but we went around a curve and almost hit the side of a building. Then I remembered."

He turned to his friend, "Joe, wasn't there a man standing back there wearing a yellow shirt?" Joe answered, "Yes, I saw him." Rog then told Joe the story his cousin had told him. Perhaps it was time to reconsider the existence of ghosts.

Rog and Joe checked around, asking questions about the boy in the yellow shirt. They were told that in the 1960s, a boy was late coming home from a date one night. He was driving too fast and was killed in the curve on Big Ridge Road. Now he tries to warn people of the dangerous curve ahead. Rog, for one, heeds the warning: "I still go that way, but when I get to that curve, I slow down...and I go slow for the rest of my trip."

Vincent Rog still isn't sure he believes in ghosts. But he is quick to admit his experience was "one hell of a coincidence."

"*I would hear the tap, tap, tap of his cane.*"

Linden

TOURISTS who have a sensation of *déjà vu* while passing through the front door of Linden shouldn't be too disturbed. After all, the beautiful doorway, which is surrounded by slender columns and an elegant fanlight, was used as the model for Tara's doorway in the motion picture *Gone With the Wind*. Built in the 1790s, Linden has always been considered one of the "ornaments" of Natchez—it was described by no less a personage than Aaron Burr as one of the "magnificent homes of gentlemen planters." Since the 1840s it has been home to the descendants of William and Jane Conner; the Feltus family, currently in residence, is the sixth generation of Conners to live in the home.

Mrs. Jeanette Feltus enjoys her role as the current Lady of Linden. She revels in the history of her home as well as in the parade of visitors that make Linden a very popular bed and breakfast inn. She is also very comfortable with the *unseen* residents of Linden. After all, they are probably just family.

Stories of ghostly happenings at Linden go back many years. "In olden days the road around Linden was graveled," Mrs. Feltus said. "Late in the afternoon, the family would sit on the back gallery. In those days, they could hear a buggy coming and could tell whose buggy it was by the way the gravel moved. People got used to the way a certain buggy sounded.

"One afternoon as they sat on the gallery, they heard the sound of a neighbor's buggy. They all said, 'That's John's buggy,' even though they knew that John had died shortly before. They waited but no one came in. Someone finally went out front and no one was there. But they had all heard the buggy come up, the horses' hooves, and someone get out of the buggy.

"When my husband, Richard, was young," she remembered, "there was a pool table upstairs. He and some of his friends were playing pool and one of the boys walked out on the backstairs gallery to wait his turn. He called and said, 'Richard, come here!' All of the boys walked out. The ghost of a lady was on the roof of the east wing. As they watched, she jumped off the roof and floated across the courtyard. Before she reached the ground, she disappeared. They talked about that for years.

"When my father-in-law, Dick, was living here," she continued, "one of his close cousins died. One night Dick awoke and saw this cousin standing at the foot of his bed. Dick said, 'Well, how are you doing?' The cousin replied, 'I'm fine. I just came back to see how things are going.' Dick was a very friendly person and he got up to shake his hand. His cousin said, 'Oh, you can't touch me.' And when Dick insisted, the cousin disappeared."

Mrs. Feltus' children also had their share of ghostly experiences. "When my children were growing up, my daughter, Celice, had two beds in her room so she would have room for company. More than one time, a girl would awake in the middle of the night and see a man with a top hat standing over them. This happened many times.

"We have a buzzer system that connects my bedroom with the children's rooms. One night Celice was alone and was washing her face in the bathroom. The mirror reflected the hall, and when she looked in the mirror, she saw something white pass through the hall. She buzzed me and I ran upstairs. All of the doors to the gallery, which had been locked with dead bolts, were wide open. The only way to open them was from the inside. I called the police, and we had six police cars out here...but we never found a thing."

———

66

he ghost of a lady was on the roof of the east wing." Linden—Front view.

"The ghosts here are friendly." Linden—Interior, 19th-Century card game.

The west wing was built in the 1840s and several years ago Mrs. Feltus was renovating it. "I was over there sewing one night," she remembered. "I started down the inside steps...*and I felt pressure on my shoulders.* I never turned around; I just kept on walking."

Mrs. Feltus is not the only person to have had a strange experience in the west wing. "When I was putting in the bathrooms, one of the plumbers came to see me," she said. "He asked, 'Mrs. Feltus, are there ghosts over there?' I said, 'Yes,' and he replied, 'Well, one of them just came.'"

Although Mrs. Feltus' father-in-law, Dick, died in the late 1970s, he still makes his presence known now and then. "Before he died, he was confined to a wheelchair, but before then, he walked with a cane for years," Jeanette Feltus said. "As old people often do, he would get up in the night and walk up and down the back gallery. I would hear the tap, tap, tap of his cane.

"Early one morning the year after he died, my little dog started barking. I made her hush, because I was afraid she would wake up the guests." Mrs. Feltus believes her dog was hearing a sound she herself could not hear but her guests could.

The next morning, all three couples who were in the same wing asked her at breakfast, "Who was walking on the gallery last night with a cane?"

Mrs. Feltus thought for a second and replied, "Oh, that was Dick."

They wanted to know, "Well, where is he?"

Mrs. Feltus quickly answered, "I guess he's in heaven." As her guests sat in stunned silence, Mrs. Feltus remembered the date. It was Dick's birthday!

"I've always heard if someone leaves this earth worried, they won't rest until their mind is relieved," she said. "I was already a widow when Dick died, and I believe he was worried about how I would carry on by myself. I think he saw, though, that everything was okay."

Mrs. Feltus is so used to unusual things happening

around the house that she hardly gives them a second thought. "We have certain doors around here that slam at a certain time every night," she said. "And I have heard noises like people talking, but I couldn't understand what they were saying. And I hear crashes every now and then.

"One time I was in the library watching television and the door opened to the hall. The tongue of the door was in the keeper, so it couldn't have opened by itself. When the door opened, a gust of wind passed through the room. Then the door closed by itself, and I heard the tongue go back in the keeper. I was glad to feel the gust of wind, though. I'd much rather that than a real human being breaking in. The ghosts here are friendly."

And what would she say to a tourist who spots Dick? "Don't worry. Dick was a perfect gentleman."

*"I felt a sudden chill. It must
have been about twenty degrees
cooler on those steps...."*

The Spengler Street Hotel

IN 1975, photographer Steve Colston bought an old
two-story building in downtown Jackson to use as his
studio. "It was in danger of being condemned and torn
down," he said. "I didn't know any of the building's history
when I bought it, except that it was built in the early 1920s
and the builder's wife still lived in the bottom right side."

Once Mr. Colston bought the building, people started
coming by and telling him stories. His building, it seemed,
had been "developing" a reputation—a violent and ghostly
one—long before he started developing photographs within
its walls.

"Back in the 1920s, this was a nice residential area—the
Belhaven area," he said. "The train that ran between Jackson and New Orleans turned around here, and a man
wanted to build a small hotel for the railroad workers. First
he had to gain the permission of the local residents. He
showed them a drawing of the proposed hotel that was
really beautiful, and everyone agreed to let him build. This
was the only commercial building in the entire area at that
time, and the building that was actually built looked nothing like the drawing. Everyone was really mad about it."

The hotel looked like something out of the old West with
its boxy construction and double front porches that were
joined with square wooden pillars. On the first floor, the
left side of the building was a café. The owners lived on the
right side. The upstairs was the "hotel" portion of the
building and was reached only by an outside set of stairs.

"I've been told it cost 30 cents for a bed—not a room,"
Colston said, "and a shower cost 10 cents extra. Most of
the people who stayed here in the early days were railroad
people.

"I know of at least three people who died violently here,"
he continued. "The owner was found dead in bed. He had
been shot in the head. It was ruled a suicide, but people in
the neighborhood said it couldn't have been suicide because he was found with one hand behind his head and
lying on the other arm. But I don't think he's the ghost.

"In the 1930s, a man who was staying here went out with
a married woman and then came back here drunk. The
woman's husband came looking for him and beat him up.
The husband stomped this guy's head in with a pair of
boots and killed him. This is who I think the ghost is.

"Then in the 1950s," Colston continued, "a man was
killed in a shoot-out in the upstairs hall. We just recently
repaired the bullet holes." In addition to these known
murders, Colston believes that other violent deaths could
possibly have occurred during the time of World War II,
when the building was used for prostitution and gambling.
At any rate, during remodeling following a flood in the late
1970s, a skeleton, complete with heavy work shoes that
lace with the help of hooks, was found at the back of the
building. The police speculated that the building had been
constructed on the site of a pauper's graveyard. But perhaps more than three murders did indeed take place at the
old hotel.

Mr. Colston's entire family pitched in to help renovate the
building. "One day my grandmother and I were downstairs,
and we heard walking upstairs. My grandmother said,
'Steve, what's your grandfather doing upstairs?' I said, 'I
don't think he is. I think he's outside washing out paint
brushes.' Sure enough, we looked out the window and my
grandfather was in the yard washing paint brushes. We
were puzzled, but we didn't think any more about it."

Even though Colston passed off the first incident, he

"She saw an image come to an upstairs front window, pull the shade back, and watch her..." Spengler Street Hotel.

continued to hear rumors that the building was haunted, and evidence to back up the stories mounted.

"I was using just the downstairs, and I had left the upstairs the way it was when I bought it," Colston said. "All of the old furniture was still in the rooms, and the windows were covered with old-fashioned shades.

"I had rented part of the downstairs to a man whose wife was an artist," Colston said. "She was working across the street painting a picture one day when she suddenly rushed into the studio. She asked her husband, 'Have you been upstairs?' He said, 'No. You can't get upstairs from in here.' Then she told us she had seen an image come to an upstairs front window, pull the shade back, and watch her as she painted. But no one was upstairs.

"I've had problems keeping the front door locked. I would lock it at night and when I came in the next morning, it would be unlocked. I thought someone was coming in, but nothing was ever missing. I took a big nail and drove it into the door facing to see if someone was coming in. Every morning the front door would still be unlocked, but the nail hadn't been disturbed."

Most of Colston's unearthly happenings are just minor annoyances, but sometimes they can be expensive. "Every light fixture in this place has fallen," he said. "The electrician says that the screws just pull out of the heavy beams for no reason. Once, falling lights crashed a 4 x 5 enlarger, and another time, they crashed a camera. The electrician says you can't put lights up better than he put them up—but they keep crashing down anyway."

Colston said that most of the phenomena take place late in the afternoon or at night. "Since I'm usually not here at night, when I hear things, it's usually about five or six in the evening. I have a pressure mat that chimes when someone comes in and steps on it. I have been *in* the room and the mat would chime. Of course, no one is there."

Colston can recount incident after incident that involves either him or his friends. "Once some friends opened a

---

pottery shop upstairs. The man would come up and work at night and go into the bathroom, and the bathroom doorknob would turn by itself and jam.

"One afternoon two guys came in and brought a camera to show me," Colston said. "One was drinking a bottled Coke and set it on the desk. While we were standing there, the bottle turned over and rolled off the desk! It hit the floor and turned and rolled straight toward the front door. All *three* of us saw that!"

A few years ago, Mr. Colston decided to install an inside staircase to connect the two floors. Until then, the only way to get to the second floor was by the outside stairs. "I rented the upstairs to a woman. She kept a bell on the doorknob of the door that led to the outside stairs, so if a customer came up that way, she would know.

"One day we were sitting down here and the bell started ringing. We knew the upstairs outside door was locked, and we hadn't seen anyone walking around outside," Colston said, "but I went out to check. No one was there and the door was still locked. I thought it must have been a breeze. I came back inside and went up the inside steps. I unlocked the door and walked down the outside steps. I felt a sudden chill. It must have been about twenty degrees cooler on those steps. The hair on my arms stood up. Later, I tried to make the bell ring without opening the door, but I couldn't."

The sounds of heavy walking on the second floor seem to be the most common phenomenon. Colston once went to the trouble and expense to carpet the upstairs—partly in hopes the sounds would stop. Instead, a new phenomenon began. It started late one afternoon when the carpet layer began work. Colston and his wife decided to go out for dinner and when they returned about an hour later, the carpet layer was sitting in his truck. Colston asked, "Are you through already?"

The man shook his head and replied, "I don't know whether you know it or not, but this place is haunted!"

"What do you mean?" Colston asked.

"I was upstairs working and I kept hearing someone talking," he replied. "I thought ya'll had come back, so I came downstairs, but no one was there."

Mr. Colston said, "I know exactly what he meant. I've heard it a lot since then. It's a muffled sound. It reminds me of being on a bus—you can hear other people talking around you, but you can't understand what they are saying."

So many incidents have occurred over the years that Colston has given up trying to keep track. "I can't remember everything. But things continue to happen. Things disappear...especially tape dispensers. A dispenser will vanish and we'll think one of us did something with it. Eventually, it will turn up right where we last saw it."

Colston doesn't mind sharing his business with a ghost, and the constant noises don't bother him. "When you live with it that long, you don't even think about it. Anyway, I kind of *like* having a haunted house."

"The Lady"—Meridian's Grand Opera House

ERIDIAN'S Grand Opera House is a magnificent tribute to the importance of Meridian and its culture in the post-Civil War South. By the turn of the century, Meridian, along with Atlanta, was one of the two largest inland cities in the South. Five railroad lines passed through the town; and the Grand Opera House, which opened in 1890, took advantage of the touring opera companies, Broadway shows, vaudeville and minstrel shows, and Shakespearean repertory companies that toured the United States by train.

The Grand Opera House is nicknamed "The Lady" because of a hand-painted portrait of a young lady on the proscenium above the stage. The term "Grand Opera House" itself wasn't a pretentious title—it was a classification. Before a theater could be designated as a Grand Opera House, it had to meet specific requirements, such as the size of the stage and the number of seats and dressing rooms. And as the highest classification, The Lady attracted the finest talent in the country.

Her stage was graced by legendary performers which included Sarah Bernhardt, Norma Shearer, and Helen Hayes. Some reports indicate that Enrico Caruso, Lon Chaney, John Gilbert, and George Gershwin also appeared. A signature, apparently written by a young man, was found underneath several layers of old wallpaper in one of the dressing rooms. It was signed "George Gershwin." Although Gershwin has never been officially documented as a performer in Meridian, it is known that he performed with touring companies in his youth.

The Lady is a magnificent example of late Victorian Empire/Romanesque architecture, and bore the distinction of being the only second-story opera house in the South. She was reached by a staircase which swept from 5th Street to the ornate second-story lobby. Elaborate gold leafing accented her white and gold walls, and her seats were upholstered in wine velvet.

After thirty-seven years of glory, the Meridian Grand Opera House closed in 1927. The staircase, her main link with the outside world, was demolished. A thriving business occupied the street-level part of the building beneath her lobby, and little remained to remind people of her presence. She was sealed, like a Pharaoh's tomb, for over sixty years.

As The Lady slumbered behind her walls, the Great Depression, World War II, the Cold War, Vietnam, Watergate, and most of the twentieth century passed. But even with the curtain down and the doors locked shut, the singing never really stopped. A lady *still* sings at the old opera house. Although several people have been aware of a presence in the theater, the ghostly lady seems to save most of her performances for younger people.

Sara and Elliot Rush, ages twelve and ten, walked into the theater one day and heard singing. "We were walking up the stairs and we heard a lady singing," said Elliot. "She was singing words, but I couldn't understand anything. The singing sounded like it was coming from the stage, but I couldn't see anything. That's why I knew she wasn't real; she was a ghost. She quit singing, and then I heard footsteps like she was walking off of the stage." "We left the building real fast," said Sara.

Unnaturally cold spots seem to be a common phenomenon around the old opera house. "I ran into a cold spot on stage once," said Fonda Rush, who is the mother of Sara and Elliot; and others have experienced cold spots in the

"The singing sounded like it was coming from the stage, but I couldn't see anything." Meridian's Grand Opera House.

backstage area. But Ms. Rush's most unusual experience at the opera house came one stormy afternoon as she guided a group of ladies on tour.

"We were standing in the auditorium and we heard shattering glass. All of us heard it," Ms. Rush said. "It sounded as though an entire window had blown out at the front of the opera house. We looked around but there was no broken window. I told Elliot Street, who is the executive director, and we went all over the opera house and never found anything broken."

In 1989, Meridian remembered her grandest lady and determined to restore her to her former splendor. The Grand Opera House of Mississippi, Inc. was formed to restore the opera house as a center for the creative and performing arts. Once again her stage will ring with the sound of laughter, orchestras, and singing.

Who is the ghostly lady of Meridian's Grand Opera House? No one even has a guess. But it is fascinating to speculate which lady from America's touring companies may have chosen to make Meridian her permanent home.

*"You can hear eighteenth-century music...
it's so clear that I get up to see if
a tourist has come by with a radio."*

Springfield

THE history of few mansions in Mississippi can compare with the intrigue and romance that still swirl around Springfield Plantation in rural Jefferson County. Springfield, built in 1790 by Thomas Marston Green, is one of the oldest major structures still standing in the entire Mississippi Valley. Its age and the fact that it is probably the first full-columned, two-story mansion to be built west of the Atlantic seaboard make it of utmost architectural importance. And a famous marriage assured Springfield of a permanent place in history.

In the spring of 1791, Andrew Jackson and Rachael Robards were married in Springfield's parlor—an event which is still a matter of hot debate with some historians. When the Jacksons married, both bride and groom believed Rachael and her first husband had been granted a divorce. Unfortunately the divorce had not been granted, and the embarrassment and harassment over their invalid Mississippi marriage would haunt the Jacksons for the rest of their lives.

In the twentieth century, Springfield suffered the neglect common to so many mansions in the Natchez area. By the 1970s, the structure was deserted and close to ruin. Springfield needed a savior. It found one in the person of Arthur La Salle, a determined descendant of the famous Mississippi River explorer, René-Robert Cavelier sieur de La Salle.

"I first read about Springfield when I was sixteen years old, and it has been my lifelong desire to preserve this

"It was a cold winter night and I realized I was the first person in eleven years to spend a night in this house." Springfield—View from parlor window.

house," Arthur La Salle said. After the owners, who lived in St. Louis, declined to sell, La Salle negotiated a lease on Springfield in return for restoring it. He sold his own historic home in Pennsylvania and moved into Springfield in 1977. He has never felt alone.

When La Salle began his restoration, he and his sons, Adam and Carl, lived in the kitchen wing. One night a friend of his sons was staying with them, and La Salle decided he had had enough of teenage companionship. "We had been camping in the kitchen wing and I finally wanted a little privacy," he remembered. "The only room sealed in the main house was the bathroom, and it was empty except for a bathtub turned upside down." There was no electricity or heat in the house as La Salle bedded down for the night.

"The kids were back in the kitchen wing, which is not a part of the main house. I made my bed on the floor of the bathroom with a kerosene heater, a kerosene lamp, and a flashlight beside me. It was a cold winter night and I realized I was the first person in eleven years to spend a night in this house.

"As soon as I turned the light out, there were heavy footsteps across the floor of the bedroom next to the bathroom. The footsteps came right up to the door of the bathroom and I thought, 'If that doorknob turns, I'm going to be upset.' I was more worried about some living intruder than about a spiritual presence."

La Salle turned on the flashlight and waited. Nothing happened. No knob turned. No heavy steps moved away from the door. "I grabbed the doorknob and opened the door," he said, "but no one was there."

La Salle has heard the same footsteps more than once, as well as a variety of other aural phenomena. "The most consistent thing is the great crash," La Salle said. "About once a year on a quiet Sunday afternoon when few people are around, there is a great crash that almost seems to shake the house. It's like an enormous piece of furniture has fallen over.

"And then there's the music," he continued. "It seems to happen on still days in the spring...*you can hear eighteenth-century music.* It's orchestral and I hear it on the west side of the house. It's so clear that I get up to see if a tourist has come by with a radio. But no one is ever there!"

When Thomas Marston Green built his mansion, the entire west side of the second floor was a ballroom. Perhaps the music that floats from the west side of Springfield is a memory of the elegant parties Green gave. Perhaps in the midst of the music, two figures still dance. Perhaps Andrew and Rachael Jackson dance to the music of their youth—deeply in love and not yet touched by the scandal brought on by their youthful impulsiveness.

"About once a year on a quiet Sunday afternoon when few people are around, there is a great crash that almost seems to shake the house." Springfield—Front view.

*"You can hear the rustling of
petticoats and smell the
strong scent of her perfume."*

The Perfumed Lady
of Lakemont

WHEN John Wayne Jabour and his wife, Becky, bought
the old William Lake home in Vicksburg in the 1970s,
they became the caretakers of both a lovely old home
and a legend—the legend of the perfumed lady.

Lakemont, as the home is known today, was originally a
two-story Greek Revival house with six cypress Doric columns spaced across a wide veranda. It was built in 1830
by William Lake, a young man on the rise. Lake was a
lawyer who would become a judge, a state senator, a U.S.
Congressman, and would be elected to the Confederate
Congress. Unfortunately he never lived to serve the Confederacy. In October of 1861, he was killed in a duel by a
political rival.

Dueling was illegal in Mississippi. According to legend as
well as family records, Judge Lake and his opponent chose
to confront each other at De Soto Point, a peninsula in the
river which was actually a part of Louisiana. Mrs. Lake
watched through a spyglass from her upstairs bedroom
window as her husband fell to the ground. He died in the
arms of his second, Captain Leathers. Mrs. Lake mourned
her husband's death until the end of her life, but many
witnesses believe she still returns to Lakemont in a swish of
petticoats and a swirl of fine perfume.

Becky Jabour believes the legend. "Late in the afternoon,
on the front gallery toward the river, there will be a sudden
hush. Things will get very still. You can hear the rustling

of her petticoats and smell the strong scent of her perfume. The fragrance is a strong, flowery odor. It's a jasmine scent, very intense, and an old-fashioned 'sweet' like your grandmother used to wear. It's definitely not a current perfume."

Both Jabours have smelled the perfume and have noticed that it usually occurs in October when nothing is blooming in the yard. "I've wondered," Mrs. Jabour said, "if it has anything to do with the fact that Judge Lake was killed in October."

The Jabours have pieced together the history of their home and have managed to trace many of the original furnishings. "It's amazing how things have fallen into place and how we have learned things," Becky Jabour said. "Years ago some friends of ours were skiing out West and they met a couple descended from the Lakes. We got in touch with them. The wife was descended from the Lakes' youngest daughter and her uncle has most of the family furnishings and paintings. He knew all about the family tree, and according to his records, William Lake was indeed killed in Vicksburg."

The Jabours also learned another interesting twist in the Lake family history. Captain Leathers, the man who was William Lake's second in the duel, lived to be an old man. He died after being hit by a bicycle on a street in New Orleans. A young boy was walking by at the time of the accident and ran over to help the old man. Captain Leathers died in his arms. The boy was William Lake's great-grandson.

Although Fisher Funeral Home records indicate that Judge Lake was killed in Memphis, Mrs. Jabour wonders if the records might be mistaken. "The family records say he was killed here in Vicksburg. At one time, I thought the funeral home records must be correct, but after I did a lot of research, including researching census records, I found that they made a lot of mistakes—a clerk just wrote down

"Right in the middle of the ghost story...the mirror cracked from side to side."
Lakemont—Cracked Federal mirror.

the wrong thing. Anyway, the legend sounds nicer," she said with a smile.

"The main point is," she continued, "that William Lake was killed in a duel, and it hurt Mrs. Lake deeply. She more or less went into seclusion. She went to Alabama for a while and then came back here where she died."

Mrs. Lake may make her presence known in other ways. Becky Jabour clearly remembers the first time Lakemont was opened to the public after it had been restored: "The first time we opened the house during Pilgrimage was in 1978. On the first morning I started giving the tour, I began my talk with the history of the house. Right in the middle of the ghost story, there was a loud crash. I thought a large platter had fallen, but when I looked, everything seemed to be all right. When we went into the parlor and I began to tell about the mirror, I saw the mirror had cracked." The gilded 1790 Federal mirror with convex curved glass had cracked from side to side. "It didn't fall; it just cracked. Nothing was different except the crack. It *totally* undid me.

"I thought, 'Maybe she isn't pleased with the restoration, or maybe she doesn't like us opening the house.' I wondered if anything else would happen, but nothing did. I think she was just making her presence known and letting us know that she was here."

Other things happen around the house as well. "There are little things," Mrs. Jabour said. "Something will pass me in the hall that feels like the wind. It's very subtle, but you know something was there. Once I was sitting on the bed reading, and as I was thinking about getting up and closing the door...it closed all by itself."

Books tend to fall out of a certain cabinet, and both Jabours have heard footsteps coming down the stairs several times. "It was very definite because the staircase creaks on a certain step. There was never anyone there. And I have heard someone walking upstairs when no one was there," Becky Jabour said.

The top floor of the house burned in 1916 and was never replaced. "The lady who lived here at the time of the fire would hear a thumping sound every night in the wall of the main bedroom. After the fire, she never heard it again," Mrs. Jabour said.

John Wayne Jabour remembered entertaining guests one night when the door to the linen press opened by itself. "We have some liquor stored in there," Mr. Jabour laughed, "and the only thing I could think was that the ghost thought it was time to give the people a drink!"

Although the Jabours have never seen their perfumed lady, they have reason to suspect she may not be their only unseen company. "One day a friend was sitting talking to me, and her face went pale," Becky Jabour remembered. "I asked her what was wrong—it was obvious something was. She said she saw a figure standing in the doorway. It was hazy, but she thought it was a man with ruffles at the neck."

The entire family takes their invisible guests in stride. "The children feel she's like a guardian angel," Mrs. Jabour said. "She's a good ghost. In a way, she's like a part of the family."

But do the Jabours *really* believe in ghosts? "Probably not, but I don't know," Becky Jabour smiles. "The longer I live here...."

Thomas Henderson's Last Message

THOMAS Henderson, a wealthy Natchez planter, cotton broker, and merchant, built Magnolia Hall in 1858. Although he chose the classic Greek Revival style so popular in Natchez during the mid-1800s, the brownstone finish of his mansion set it apart from the other white-clad palaces of the wealthy. Henderson had a lot in common with many of the other builders of Natchez' magnificent mansions—he had precious little time to enjoy his creation.

In January of 1863, Thomas Henderson suffered a paralyzing stroke which kept him confined in a downstairs bedroom until his death two months later. His daughter Julia, like many well-educated Southern women of her time, kept a diary. In it she recorded those difficult months, including her father's desperate, unsuccessful attempts to convey a message during the weeks before his death.

Today, Magnolia Hall is owned by the Natchez Garden Club which maintains the first floor much as it was in Henderson's lifetime. The second floor serves as a museum which houses a collection of eighteenth- and nineteenth-century furniture, a textile collection, and an exhibit of pilgrimage costumes. For years the hostesses at Magnolia Hall ushered thousands of tourists through Thomas Henderson's home as they recited sterile facts from the life of a man dead over one hundred years. He was just a page from history, long dead and long forgotten, except for the elegant mansion he left behind. Then in the mid-1980s,

Thomas Henderson became more than just a name from the past.

For Judy Grimsley, a hostess at Magnolia Hall, the inexplicable began on a cool, dull day in October of 1985. "I always come to work early and I have a routine I go through, such as turning on lights and so forth," she said. "As I stepped into the downstairs bedroom, I noticed an indentation in the pillow. It was obviously made by a head. I didn't touch it. Myra Jones is our housekeeper and I have known her since we were fifteen. She is meticulous. I knew Myra wouldn't have done that."

Ms. Grimsley waited until Kay McNeil McGehee, who was the caretaker and also a hostess at Magnolia Hall, arrived. She showed Ms. McGehee the indentation. Both agreed the housekeeper would never have left the pillow in that condition, but neither had an explanation. "We fluffed the pillows back up and didn't pay any more attention to it," Ms. Grimsley said.

The weather continued cold and rainy. "On the last day of pilgrimage, we were giving the history of the house to a group of tourists," Ms. Grimsley continued. "We never tell them that Thomas Henderson died in the downstairs bedroom because it upsets some people. Unknown to us, a psychic was in the group that day. As she stepped into the bedroom, the lamp went on and off three times. The psychic said, 'Something happened in this room that no one told me about.'"

At that point Ms. McGehee began to tell the woman about Mr. Henderson, and the psychic said, "Wait, don't tell me any more. He was paralyzed and could not speak. *He was trying to say something that started with an 'm'.* He's not at rest because he never got to say those words." She asked the startled hostesses if there was anything in the room that had belonged to Henderson. One of the hostesses handed her a small leather-bound Bible. It had belonged to Thomas Henderson's father, John.

As the psychic held the Bible, it fell open to a chapter in

Exodus where God told Moses to convey a message. When she handed the Bible back to a hostess, it was so hot the hostess had to put it down. By that time, quite a crowd had gathered in the room and several of the hostesses tried to pick up the book. "I tried," said Ms. Grimsley, "but it was too hot to touch. And there was no way that sunlight could have come through a window and heated the book. That day was very overcast; no sun was shining whatsoever. The woman kept talking, telling us things about Mr. Henderson that she couldn't possibly know, and eventually the Bible cooled enough to be picked up. It was eerie."

After this episode, Ms. McGehee began to talk of her experiences at Magnolia Hall—experiences that until then she hadn't mentioned. As caretaker, she lived at the back of the mansion in the servants' wing with her two cats. Sometimes, in the middle of the night, the cats would bristle in front of the door. She also heard noises that sounded like pictures sliding off the walls, but the next morning she could not find anything to explain the strange noises.

Perhaps Mr. Henderson was stirring things up a bit on his way to the kitchen. Ms. Grimsley believes he still enjoys an occasional late night snack. "We have records that tell us Mr. Henderson was fond of midnight snacks," she said. "He would come into the kitchen and fix the food himself so he wouldn't have to disturb the servants. We have recently found evidence of food in the kitchen when we open early in the morning, and there is no way that someone could come in here and eat. It's definitely *not* a mouse," she emphasized.

Ms. Grimsley may have seen the ghost of Mr. Henderson early one morning. "I came in very early and had gone through my ritual of turning the lights on when I stepped out the front door to adjust the signs. I had the feeling that someone was watching me," she said. "I turned around and in the hall behind me, I saw a distinct shape on the stairs. It was gray. I did a double-take, and it disap-

"As she stepped into the bedroom, the lamp went on and off three times. The psychic said, 'Something happened in this room that no one told me about.'"
Magnolia Hall—Thomas Henderson's bedroom.

peared. And I had not been partying the night before," she added with a laugh.

The sounds of walking are common. Also the odor of laudanum, a popular nineteenth-century medicine made from opium, is occasionally smelled in one of the upstairs bedrooms. But perhaps the strangest phenomenon that occurs on a continuing basis at Magnolia Hall is the appearance of large rocks on a bedroom floor. "It's not the pea gravel we have outside," Ms. Grimsley said. "These are rocks, about six inches across. We throw them away, but in a few months they reappear."

Why rocks? Several possible explanations have been offered. "One man told me that the ghost wants you to sleep like a rock," Ms. Grimsley said. "Another suggested the ghost wants you to dig for minerals or treasure."

Was this what Thomas Henderson was trying to convey during his last days on earth? That something starting with the letter "m" was buried nearby? Metal? Minerals? Unless Henderson finds a better way of communicating, we may never know.

In the meantime, Judy Grimsley and the other hostesses at Magnolia Hall take the ghostly happenings in good (shall we say?) spirits. "Once we had these things to occur, we started laughing about it," Ms. Grimsley said. "We said, 'Oh well, Longwood has a ghost, and Dunleith has a ghost, so we will just have a ghost also.' Seriously," she added, "this isn't something you make up."

*A definite indentation, the size of
a small child, would appear on the
canopied bed in the afternoon.*

Waverly's Lonely Child

ROBERT and Donna Snow of Philadelphia, Mississippi,
heard tales of a magnificent mansion standing deserted
deep within the woods around West Point. Wondering
if anything could be as regal as the rumors indicated, they
set out to see for themselves. After crossing a river by ferry
and hacking their way through tangled undergrowth, they
caught their first glimpse of Waverly.

The massive four-story structure, which had been built in
1852, had been abandoned for fifty years. White paint was
peeling from its huge columns, and dozens of shutters
hung askew from windows or lay scattered about the
grounds. Vines had climbed up its sides and curled
through broken windows. Birds and bats had made the
lofty octagonal cupola their home for years, and their resi-
due covered the floors along with leaves, branches, cob-
webs, and the litter of hundreds of human curiosity seek-
ers. Graffiti covered every square inch of the plastered
walls. It was a magnificent mess.

As Mrs. Snow carefully picked her way across the rotting
front porch, her husband looked at her and said, "Donna,
we've just got to buy this house." She looked at him in
amazement and replied, "You have *got* to be crazy."

But she knew he was right. Beneath the decay and
peeling paint, Waverly was majestic. "There was no furniture, no curtains, and birds and bats were everywhere," she
remembered, "but it was the most gorgeous piece of architecture I had ever seen."

The Snows realized they had found a forgotten master-piece. Waverly was the only pre-Civil War home to have a second, third, and fourth-story balcony overlooking the main floor. Twin circular cantilevered staircases, with railings comprised of over seven hundred spindles, rose four floors to an octagonal cupola sixty-five feet above the rotunda. Exquisite millwork and ornamental plaster graced the walls and ceilings throughout the house. Decades of vandals had miraculously left intact the imported French brass chandeliers, gilded mirrors, and marble mantels. The Snows decided to restore Waverly to its former magnifi-cence, or in Donna Snow's words, "We decided, as the younger generation says, 'to do our thing.'" Their efforts have been duly recognized. Waverly is now a National Historic Landmark.

The Snows moved their family into the huge house and embarked on a massive restoration process. Fortunately, even though the home was in disrepair, it was structurally sound. The Snows and their four children sometimes lived in a single room as other areas were restored. Slowly, room by room, Waverly was painstakingly brought back from the edge of ruin.

During the restoration, thoughts of the supernatural never crossed Donna Snow's mind, even though the family's sleep was disturbed night after night by loud noises. "Al-most every night, we would be awakened by crashing noises that sounded as if the entire ceiling had fallen in." Since they lived near an air base, they checked out the possibility of sonic booms, but they could never find any reason for the loud, disturbing noises. Finally the noises stopped. Even though they never found a logical explana-tion for the crashing sounds, the supernatural still just wasn't a part of their reality.

"Goodness knows, this house did look like a ghost house when we first saw it, but never in my wildest dreams did I ever think there was anything here," Donna Snow said. "We had been here about two years, never dreaming that

"Almost every night, we would be awakened by crashing noises that sounded as if the entire ceiling had fallen in." Waverly—Front view.

anything supernatural had ever roamed this earth, when I was cleaning upstairs one afternoon. Right at my feet, this angelic little girl's voice, very sweetly, said, 'Mama? Mama?' It was so close, I could have touched her." Mrs. Snow looked, but no one was there. Puzzled, she thought she must have heard a bird.

The next afternoon, in a different room, she heard the same sweet voice calling, "Mama? Mama?" Day after day, Mrs. Snow heard the child calling for her mother. She finally came to terms with the fact that Waverly held not just her four children within its walls, but five. One child was a ghost who constantly searched for her mother.

Mrs. Snow heard the child for about two years. Then she discovered that during the afternoon, something about the size of a three-year-old child was sleeping upstairs in one of the large canopied beds. A definite indentation, the size of a small child, would appear on the bed in the afternoon. "You could see the indentation on the bed. You could touch it and it was neither warm nor cold, and it would remain there until late in the afternoon when it disappeared. One day, we went to the room and stayed all afternoon. We talked normally but did not take our eyes off that bed. A little after 4:30, right before our eyes, the bed straightened up completely. We didn't hear a thing."

Then one afternoon, about eighteen years ago, Mrs. Snow heard the ghost child for the last time. "Instead of sweetly calling, she raised her voice loudly, like a frightened child, and screamed, 'Mama!' about five times. That day, I impulsively answered her and said, 'I really want to help you if you will tell me what I can do for you.' She didn't call again after that day, and she quit sleeping on her bed."

During the ten years that followed, Mrs. Snow often wondered what happened to the lonely little girl who searched so hard for her mother. There was an indication, however, that she had not left. On one occasion a Scottish couple was touring Waverly. As the woman left, she turned to Mrs. Snow and said, "Oh, you have a spirit in the

---

house." Mrs. Snow answered, "No, we don't. We used to have one, a little girl, but she left." The lady replied, "You have a spirit in the house today. I can sense it." Soon after, for no apparent reason, the little girl started sleeping on her bed again.

Even though she is no longer heard, the ghost child has been seen since her return by both Mrs. Snow and her daughter, Cindy. She is, indeed, a small child about three years of age. Mrs. Snow saw the child in 1990. "About 10:30 one night a little girl was standing on the stairwell that goes to the third floor. I only saw her from the side. She had dark blonde hair that fell beneath her shoulders, and she was wearing a long nightgown with a high neck. It didn't scare me because I had known for years that she was here, but it startled me. I stopped and looked at her. When I did, she began to slowly dissolve into a cloud of faint white smoke which then disappeared."

Mrs. Snow tried to discover the identity of the ghost child with no success. The builder of Waverly, George Hamilton Young, and his wife had ten children, but none died as children. She speculates that perhaps the ghost child is a granddaughter of the Youngs, although she emphasizes that is pure speculation. There simply are no records, and the identity of the child remains a mystery.

Other than indentations on the bed and rare appearances on the staircase, Waverly's sad little ghost seems to be very quiet. She never makes noises or moves things...well, almost never. There *is* the mystery of the missing peach pickle spoon. Mrs. Snow has a special sterling peach pickle spoon which she uses on festive family occasions. One year between Christmas and Thanksgiving, it disappeared. She searched for days and could not imagine what had happened to it. Months later, Cindy retrieved a flow blue bowl from a high shelf in a display case. Something was rattling inside; it was the sterling spoon. Suspicion fell on the little girl ghost. "I just think she took a liking to that spoon," Donna Snow smiled.

Today, the little girl ghost still sleeps in her bed, although some tourists have seen an indentation that looks more like a small child sitting on the side of the bed. But she never calls for her mother. Perhaps Mrs. Snow's concern gave her the reassurance she needed. Perhaps she found the companionship she was searching for in the presence of the Snow family and the thousands of people who come every year to visit her at Waverly.

"A little girl was standing on the stairwell that goes to the third floor...she began to slowly dissolve into a faint cloud of white smoke." Waverly—Staircase between second and third floors.

"It was transparent, but it was shaped like a woman and it was coming in my direction!"

Chapel of the Cross

MANY Mississippians consider the story of Helen Johnstone, who will be forever known as "The Bride of Annandale," to be the most romantic of our ghost stories. The story of Helen's misfortune in love is entwined with the history of Annandale and the Chapel of the Cross.

Annandale was a huge Madison County mansion planned in the 1840s by John Johnstone after the style of the Scottish castle owned by his ancestors. Johnstone died before his mansion was built, but his wife, Margaret, fulfilled his dream. She also donated ten acres to the Episcopal diocese and built an exquisite chapel in his memory, the Chapel of the Cross.

Helen Johnstone, the daughter of John and Margaret Johnstone, was a young lady of exceptional beauty and charm. During Christmas of 1855, she met the only man she would ever love, handsome and dashing Henry Grey Vick. Vick came from a prominent Vicksburg family; in fact, the town was named for his father. Helen captured Vick's heart and he asked for her hand in marriage.

Since Helen was only sixteen, Mrs. Johnstone insisted on a long courtship. The couple agreed and a long, happy romance followed during which they discussed their fondest hopes and greatest fears. Helen was deeply religious and had strong feelings about the senselessness of duels. Duels, although illegal in most places, were still a popular way of settling differences between gentlemen. Helen believed duels were nothing short of murder, and she extracted

Vick's sworn promise he would never kill another man in a duel.

Helen and Henry Vick announced their wedding date. They were to be married on May 21, 1859 at the Chapel of the Cross. The entire county was caught up in a frenzy of anticipation and preparation. Helen was loved by the entire community and her wedding was an event to be celebrated.

A few days before the ceremony, Vick made a business trip to New Orleans. While he was there, he became involved in an argument and was challenged to a duel. In antebellum society, a gentleman could not refuse and remain a gentleman. On May 16, 1859, the day before the duel, Henry Vick wrote his will leaving a good portion of his estate to his fiancé, Helen Johnstone. Then Vick and his opponent traveled by boat to Mobile where the duel would take place.

Although Vick was obligated to defend his honor, he could not forget his vow to Helen. When the duel began, Henry Grey Vick raised his gun and fired into the air—thus fulfilling his promise never to kill a man in a duel. His opponent, however, took careful, deadly aim and shot Vick through the heart.

At Helen's request, Vick's body was brought to Madison County. He was buried during a bizarre midnight funeral in the cemetery behind the Chapel of the Cross. Some accounts say Helen wore her wedding gown to the funeral.

Helen vowed never to love another man. But after years of traveling in Europe, she returned to Madison County and married Dr. George Harris, the young rector of the Chapel of the Cross. It was to be an unusual marriage. Helen told her future husband that she would marry him, but she would never love him. She could never love anyone but Henry Grey Vick.

Helen lived to be an old woman, but her thoughts always revolved around her lost love. On her deathbed in 1916, she gasped, "He's coming back—he's coming back for me," and died with a smile on her face.

_____

Helen Johnstone Harris is buried in Rolling Fork beside her husband, but generations of Mississippians believe that Helen haunts the Chapel of the Cross, still mourning her lost love.

Even though almost one hundred and fifty years have passed since the Chapel of the Cross was built, it still stands in a quiet, rural setting. Its serene atmosphere seems to make it an unlikely host for the variety of psychic phenomena that have been reported for many years. More than one ghost inhabits the chapel and its grounds, but the most common sighting is that of Helen, The Bride of Annandale.

Several ghosts are said to inhabit the chapel itself. A ghostly male figure looming over the pulpit has been seen by several people late at night. Filmy figures have been seen opening heavy wooden doors and passing through locked iron gates, and unearthly faces have been seen peering from the chapel's windows.

One of the most persistent phenomena is organ music which floats from the locked church late at night. Generations of teenagers have passed the church at midnight hoping to hear the ghostly music.

Several years ago, Steve Colston's friend was the custodian of the church. Vandals were a problem at that time, and Mr. Colston would help his friend keep an eye on the church at night. "We would be sitting there and all of a sudden, the gate would start squeaking for no reason," Mr. Colston remembered. "There wasn't any wind or anything. The custodian said it happened all the time. He had also seen a white image move about the graveyard and then sit on a bench close to Henry Vick's grave."

The ghost of Helen has been seen by dozens, perhaps hundreds, of visitors to the chapel. One visitor was Brenda Traylor who came by the chapel late one night with friends. She had heard the ghost stories but, "I didn't believe a word of it," she said. She later changed her mind.

"It was about midnight," she remembered, "and I was

walking behind the chapel and to the right of the graveyard. I wasn't scared because I didn't believe in ghosts. It was a beautiful moonlit night and I had wandered away from my friends. Suddenly, a movement caught my eye and I looked to my left. *A white filmy shape was drifting over the graveyard.* It was transparent, but it was shaped like a woman and it was coming in my direction!

"I just ran," she said. "I took off through the woods on my right and came out about half a mile down the road. I was covered with bramble scratches. I'll never go back to that place at night!" Ms. Traylor was convinced she had seen "The Bride of Annandale." "I can't think of another explanation," she said.

During daylight hours, the chapel serves as a peaceful retreat. At night, however, it is quite another story. Its residents don't care for visitors. The cautious respect their wishes.

McLemore gasped, "I'm killed!"
as he dropped to the floor in
a spreading pool of blood.

The Knight Over Devil's Den

THE Deason Home in Ellisville sits under the spreading
branches of ancient oaks. It was built in 1845 by
Amos Deason, one of the wealthiest citizens of Jones
County. Later additions hide the home's original structure
and certainly give no hint of the intrigue and murder that
took place inside its walls. But the house
remembers...from a spreading blood stain that will not
fade, and a door that opens on a fateful anniversary, to an
empty rocking chair that rocks on still summer
afternoons...the house remembers its part in the history of
Jones County.

At the time of the Civil War, Jones County was sparsely
settled with poor farmers. In contrast to some areas in the
South, Jones Countians owned few slaves. And in a state
where cotton was the backbone of the economy, Jones
County produced only 633 bales in 1860. When the fires of
secession began burning, Jones Countians refused to
become embroiled. They instructed their delegate to the
secession convention in Jackson to vote against withdraw-
ing from the Union. But once in Jackson, their delegate
became overwhelmed with the fiery, eloquent demands for
secession and voted with the secessionists. His furious
neighbors hanged him in effigy.

Grudgingly, Jones County prepared for war. Amos
Deason also prepared for the war—by burying his gold on
his property for safekeeping.

Jones County, always a poor county where many of the people went barefoot year-round, became even poorer during the war. The young men who tilled the fields were off with the Army, and the old men, women, and children who were left behind struggled to survive. Adding to what was fast becoming a desperate situation was the Confederate Cavalry, whose job it was to feed the army. They descended on Jones County, taking food and farm animals from people who had little to give.

At the beginning of the war, some Jones County men joined the Confederacy, but others refused until the draft was instituted in 1862. One who refused was a devout hardshell Baptist farmer named Newt Knight. Knight refused to fight for a cause he did not believe in; but, once drafted, he served as a hospital orderly.

Discontent reached the breaking point among some Jones County soldiers when they discovered that if a man owned twenty or more slaves, he could avoid military service. To this group of Jones Countians, which included Knight, the discovery proved the suspicion they had harbored since the beginning of the war: it was a "rich man's war and a poor man's fight." Newt Knight went home.

Knight banded together with other deserters and formed a renegade company which hid out in caves deep within the Leaf River Swamp. Their hideout, known as the Devil's Den, was headquarters for over a hundred Confederate deserters. They came out to plow their fields, visit with their families, and according to legend, conduct raids, especially on trains headed to and from Mobile. The men communicated by hunting horns and devised an elaborate system of signals to deliver messages and warn of danger.

The danger was real. Despite a large number of deserters, most Jones County citizens were loyal Confederates. To them Newt Knight was a criminal, and they were humiliated by the actions of Knight and his renegades. They refused to grant him a safe harbor. In addition, the Confederacy was determined to capture Knight and his men.

As they stood in front of the roaring blaze, Newt Knight threw open the door and shot McLemore at point blank range. Deason House—Murder room.

Group after group tramped into the Piney Woods and trudged through the Leaf River Swamp hunting Knight and his followers with no success. Finally, the Confederacy sent Major Amos McLemore, a native of Jones County, to capture Knight.

McLemore was a formidable adversary, since he knew the Leaf River Swamp almost as well as Knight. McLemore was determined to capture Knight and was getting dangerously close to the group's hideout. Something drastic, Knight decided, must be done. McLemore must be killed.

Mr. and Mrs. Amos Deason were known throughout Jones County as loyal Confederates. They often allowed soldiers to stay with them. Mrs. Deason, on at least one occasion when Yankees were in the area, hid a Confederate soldier behind the secret panel next to a fireplace. Knight discovered that McLemore was staying with the Deasons. He and several of his men drew straws to see who would kill McLemore. Knight did not draw the short straw—but he decided that no one but he should have the dubious honor.

The September day Knight chose for the murder had been cool and rainy. After a long, wet day tramping through the swamps, McLemore and his men returned to the Deason's home and built a fire. As they stood in front of the roaring blaze, Newt Knight threw open the door and shot McLemore at point-blank range. McLemore gasped, "I'm killed!" as he dropped to the floor in a spreading pool of blood. McLemore's companions raced out the door after Knight, but he had disappeared into the rainy evening.

McLemore's blood seeped deep into the wide pine flooring of the Deason's home. Scrubbing after scrubbing finally made the stain fade, but it would return on damp evenings. After many years of enduring the bloodstained floor, descendants of the Deasons finally covered the pine boards with new wood flooring. But they could not prevent the front door from suddenly swinging open on the anniversary of the murder to reveal an empty, silent porch. Nor could they stop the rocking chair on the front porch from rocking on still summer afternoons as the ghost of Amos Deason rocks—still guarding his buried gold from invaders.

In 1991, descendants of Amos Deason gave the home to the local chapter of the Daughters of the American Revolution. They are restoring the home and opening it to the public. Several members of the DAR avoid being alone in the house. "I feel strange," one said. "It's like someone is watching me. And doors will open by themselves."

The ladies are also considering removing the new flooring. Will they find a blood stain? Many believe they will.

" ...it wasn't a reflection...my hand went right through her."

Jeff Knight's Companion from the Past

JEFF Knight often looks as though he just stepped out of the pages of a history book. Slim and lithe with long curling dark hair and dressed in a buckskin jacket, he looks more like a son of Daniel Boone than a modern teenager from Petal. As a descendant of the infamous Newt Knight of Jones County, Jeff is acutely aware of his link with history—and he has had an experience which seems to blur the lines between the past and the present.

Jeff and his family are avid Civil War reenactors and often travel to encampments where battles from the past are re-created. In April of 1991, Jeff, his mother Sylvia, his Aunt Dianne, and his sister Stephanie were attending a reenactment near Selma, Alabama. On their way, they noticed a beautiful old church sitting off the highway in the splendid isolation of the Alabama countryside. The Episcopal church, built during the years 1853 and 1854, was a beautiful example of Gothic Revival architecture with its steeply pitched roof and long narrow windows with pointed arches. The wooden church, painted barn red, had an adjoining cemetery which was surrounded by a black iron fence. The Knights were fascinated and decided they would have to investigate the church in the future.

The last morning of the reenactment, Jeff awoke feeling restless. Something was bothering him...something he didn't understand. He had planned to participate in that afternoon's battle, but he felt a compelling urge to head home. He convinced his family to pile into the van and head west.

As the church came into view, they discussed stopping but couldn't see a road leading to the church. "Something just told me to turn," Jeff remembered, "and sure enough, the road was there. We pulled over by the church, barely off the narrow road, with the driver's side on a slight downward angle. When I got out of the van, I felt as though something was pulling me toward the cemetery." Jeff walked to the rear of the cemetery, always looking over his shoulder. "I felt someone was behind me. I turned and looked and no one was there...but it felt as though something grabbed my hand."

Jeff beat a hasty retreat to the van to wait for the rest of his family. As he waited, he heard the sound of laughter, but when he checked on the group, they were silently admiring the church.

He saw a truck coming down the road and realized he would have to close the door of the van in order for it to pass. Before he could reach for the handle, the door, defying both gravity and common sense, slammed shut! Startled, Jeff said nothing as the family settled into their seats and they began to head toward home.

"As we were going down the highway," Jeff said, "I kept feeling that someone was in the back seat. Also, I kept feeling someone playing with my ear. My sister was sitting in the chair beside me, and my mother was sitting in the chair behind her. I looked and Aunt Dianne was dozing in the seat behind me. I turned back around, but the feeling didn't leave. Then I looked in the rearview mirror and saw an outline, like a shadow. *It was a girl.* She had on a cape like Little Red Riding Hood might wear which covered most of her face, and I could only see the bottom part. I kept on looking. I moved my hand in front of the shape while I was watching in the mirror to make sure it wasn't a reflection or anything like that. *My hand went right through her!*"

Jeff's family began noticing his unusual behavior. Sylvia Knight remembered, "He'd look in the rearview mirror, then turn and look...over and over. I said, 'Jeff, what's wrong?'

Jeff Knight looks more like a son of Daniel Boone than a modern teenager.
Knight as seen through a window of the Deason House.

He only replied, 'Something keeps blowing in my ear.' It wasn't until after we were home that he said, 'Mama, something got in the van with us back there.'"

That night Jeff decided to visit his girlfriend. On the way home in his truck, he was chilly and decided to roll up the window on the passenger's side. Rather than stop the truck, he reached across the seat and as he did, the window began to roll up by itself. "I just turned my head and ignored it. I figured I must be asleep. Then I felt the seat beside me sink as if someone was sitting there. I turned and looked and she was smiling at me! She had pulled the hood off her head and was smiling. She was about seventeen, had long blonde hair and green eyes, but I could see *through* her. I just turned the radio up and kept on going. I was really spooked! I was to the point of stopping my truck and getting out and walking home. I didn't feel like sticking around."

Jeff has learned to accept his companion, who shows no signs of leaving; he believes she wants to protect him. In an incident shortly after the Selma trip, he could have been seriously injured when an out-of-control truck sped toward him. Suddenly, with no explanation, the truck lost power and came to a screeching halt inches from Jeff's truck.

Sylvia Knight has also accepted the fact that she may have a permanent houseguest. Two months after the trip to Alabama, she saw a shadow in her kitchen. She asked Jeff, "Is she still with you?" Jeff answered, "Yes." She then asked, "Is she in this house right now?" When Jeff again answered, "Yes," his mother explained, "I just saw a shadow in the kitchen."

Why would Jeff's companion choose him? He thinks he may have an answer. He was in such a hurry to leave the reenactment that when they stopped at the church, he was still dressed in period clothing. Many of the tombstones in the cemetery date from the Civil War era, and Jeff believes his companion may have lost her love in the war. Who knows? Jeff may even resemble the man she loved—and lost. Perhaps she believes she has finally found him.

"...a mist started coming out of the grave and a woman's figure appeared."

Carolyn Neault's Family Legacy

WE'RE part Irish and part Indian on my mother's side of the family," said Carolyn Neault, "and my grandmother always believed that's the reason we're so psychic." Ms. Neault, a native of Columbus, grew up in a family in which psychic experiences were common occurrences, and she has a wealth of stories that involve dozens of members of her family.

Ms. Neault's great-grandfather, whom she always referred to as "Grandpa," was a shrimper for many years on the Mississippi Gulf Coast. He built his own boat, and during his lifetime *The Black Falcon* was moored at the harbor in Gulfport. As a fisherman, Grandpa always kept one eye on the weather; both his livelihood and his life depended on being able to recognize the approach of a bad storm.

Grandpa still keeps a weather eye. Even though he died in 1945, he has not forgotten his great love for the Mississippi coast and the men who make their living in boats. When the weather gets stormy, old-timers keep an eye on Grandpa's old boat slip in Gulfport. If a hurricane is truly imminent, he appears in whichever shrimp boat is moored in his former space, ringing the bell—a warning that a hurricane, not a mere squall, is on its way.

Grandpa keeps an eye on his family as well. In 1969, Ms. Neault's cousin was living with her three children in Tennessee. A nearby dam broke in the middle of the night and water washed through her home. The entire house was engulfed. Believing all three of her children were dead (her two daughters did die, but her baby son was saved because his mattress floated), the cousin was struggling to climb a tree and was losing to the rapidly rising water. Just as she was about to give up, she saw the figure of Grandpa coming across the water! Whether from exhaustion, grief, or fright, she fainted. When she awoke, she was in the top of the tree. "I'm not afraid of drowning," Ms. Neault said. "I suppose if I ever get in trouble, Grandpa will be there."

Ms. Neault also believes her great-grandfather never really left his wife. "My grandmother said my great-grand-mother and great-grandfather were always together even after he died. My grandmother *saw* him. She walked over to her mother's house one night and stopped when she got to the gate because Grandpa was standing on the porch. My great-grandmother was talking to him. Grandmother must have made a noise, because he disappeared. She walked on up to the porch and great-grandmother said, 'You saw your daddy.' My grandmother answered, 'Yes,' and great-grandmother said, 'Well, he comes home.'"

Ms. Neault's great-grandmother also remembered the time her husband appeared to her while she was visiting her sister in Texas. "Doll, you've got to go home," he said. She answered, "No, I just got here." He repeated, "You've got to go home." The next morning she learned her son, Herman, had had a heart attack, and she had to go home and help care for him.

Herman, Ms. Neault's great-uncle, was a special person in her life. For many years, he lived and worked on Ship Island.

If any piece of land in Mississippi deserves to be haunted, Ship Island ranks at the top of the list. As early as the 1500s, Ship Island was the gateway to the Missis-sippi River for European explorers. When settlers began coming from Europe, the island became a point of immigra-tion for many nationalities. Early in our state's history, it became important as a strategic military outpost, and Fort

Massachusetts was built as part of our coastal defense system during the mid-1800s. Union forces occupied the island during the Civil War and used it as a prisoner of war camp. Following the Civil War, Ship Island was used as a quarantine station, primarily to stop the spread of yellow fever.

Now, both Ship Island and Fort Massachusetts are a part of the Gulf Islands National Seashore and are under the supervision of the United States National Park Service. Ms. Neault's great-uncle Herman was once the caretaker for Ship Island. He and his wife lived in the old quarantine station since it was the only livable house on the island. But they were not alone.

"Each afternoon, the back door of the quarantine station would open and then shut," Ms. Neault said. "Uncle Herman would hear heavy footsteps going up the staircase. The steps would go into one of the bedrooms and stop. He wouldn't hear anything else. He always said, 'I don't believe in ghosts...but I don't know what it is.'

"Uncle Herman had to patrol at night. He had a dog that followed him everywhere—everywhere except the fort. The dog wouldn't go in the fort and didn't even like to go near it. He would get nervous about five o'clock every afternoon at the quarantine station, but he simply wouldn't go near the fort."

Ms. Neault's aunt loved to walk on the beach at Ship Island at night and often saw the figure of a lady walking around the lighthouse. Sometimes she couldn't see the lady but would detect a white glow moving around the lighthouse area.

Uncle Herman explored Ship Island and the other nearby islands during his lifetime. He would save small treasures for Ms. Neault, mostly artifacts from the Civil War, and bring these to her when he came to visit. Once he found a small cache of French gold coins dating from the 1640s on Cat Island. State historians have told Ms. Neault that those coins are the only physical evidence left that the French were ever there.

Uncle Herman paid Ms. Neault one last visit. "One New Year's Eve morning, I woke up talking to my uncle," Ms. Neault remembered. "He was hugging me and telling me goodbye and that he would see me again. Then the phone rang and it was my aunt telling me he had passed away that morning. He had come to tell me goodbye before he left."

Ghostly lore is found on her father's side of the family as well. "A cousin tells the story that during the Depression, his grandfather knew of a grave where a woman was buried with her jewels," Ms. Neault remembered. "He hired three men to help him dig into the grave, but as soon as the first shovel hit the ground, a mist started coming out of the grave and a woman's figure appeared. That was the beginning and ending of his grave-digging career."

The house Ms. Neault lived in as a child was also haunted. Her father had built the house on property he purchased when an old man died. Ms. Neault wonders if the ghost was the old man, keeping an eye on things. All through her childhood, she was aware of an unseen presence. "Occasionally, I would sleep on the couch in the living room. I love thunderstorms, and one night I had the front door open during one, enjoying the fury. Suddenly, someone invisible sat down with me. I ran and got in bed with my sister," Ms. Neault laughed.

The ghost seemed to have a high standard of behavior which he expected Ms. Neault to live up to. "I decided to experiment with cigarettes. We had a fireplace, and you could smoke and the chimney would pull up the smoke. I was sitting in front of the fireplace, puffing away, and I got this horrible feeling that someone was watching me and not liking what he was seeing. I knew he was upset with me." Ms. Neault put out the cigarette; that was the end of her experiment. "Another time," she added, "a boy had stayed out on the porch with me too long and I got the idea that he was mad."

When Ms. Neault's future husband, Ben, came along, he was a no-nonsense Maine native who did not believe in even the possibility of ghosts. He changed his mind. "One night we were sitting in the living room and heard footsteps but no one was there," Ms. Neault said. "Then a Dr. Pepper bottle went flying across the room.

"Although I never actually saw the ghost, my brother did, but he didn't tell me until years later. He said the ghost was an old man and he would see him in his bedroom every night."

In 1968, Ms. Neault's father bought his brother's farm. On the property was a two-story log house which Ms. Neault believes dated back to before the 1830s. The second story, which had been sealed off for many years, consisted of two large rooms separated by a breezeway. Members of the family heard walking in the breezeway and named the ghost "George." "Once we put a tape recorder in there and taped footsteps, but when the steps got close to the recorder and were the loudest, the tape broke."

Ms. Neault's father began to remodel the house, but he decided the foundation was too deteriorated and the house would have to be demolished. Timbers from the old house were salvaged and used to build a new house. It seems that George moved into the new house and has settled in his new home quite comfortably. "I don't go upstairs at night," Ms. Neault said. "There are places in the house that are cool like there's air-conditioning on. I think George is still there.

"Once I took a Ouija board upstairs and said I wanted to talk to George. The board said, 'My name isn't George; it's *Thomas.*'" Ms. Neault found that a Thomas Lipscomb lived in the house before the Civil War and a family of Thomases lived there during the 1880s and 1890s. So although the possibilities have been narrowed, the exact identity of the ghost remains a mystery.

Ms. Neault's children, Brian and Jessie, seem to have inherited her special gifts. When he was two, Brian began telling her about the cookie monster in his room. Ms. Neault assumed it was a child's nightmare until one night she woke to hear a dog coming down the hallway. "I could hear his nails clicking on the wooden floor. He came by my bed and I could hear him panting. I thought, 'Oh dear, someone left the door open and a dog got in the house.'

"I flipped on the light, but nothing was there. I finally determined that Brian's cookie monster was the dog. After asking around, I found that the woman who used to live in the house had a big boxer who watched over her."

Even the house Ms. Neault and her family occupies now has a resident ghost. "My house is only twelve years old and we've been there ten years. I didn't think anything could be there. I had grown up with ghosts and I was tired of them.

"But my daughter, Jessie, began to notice that our dog, Christie, would be looking at the doorway that led into the hall, watching, paying attention to something Jessie couldn't see. One afternoon, Jessie was in the house by herself and the dog jumped off the couch and stood in the hall, tilting her head like she was watching something. When Jessie got up to look, she saw a woman come out of my room and walk straight into the air-conditioning vent in the wall. Jessie has seen the woman several times and Brian has seen her, too."

When Ms. Neault wonders if her family's imagination has gotten the best of them, she only has to remember an experience Brian had when he was working at a local business.

"Brian began hearing people in the building when he was working at night by himself," she remembered. "He went looking for the source and when he checked out the basement, he saw people playing pool. He could see the smoke rising from the cigarettes, the shadows the lights made, and he could hear the clicking of the billiard balls."

When Brian related his experience to his mother, she answered, "No, Brian, you've got the wrong building. The billiard room was two doors down." Brian was emphatic, "No, I saw them...I swear it," and described what he saw in detail.

Years later, Ms. Neault happened to be going through a stack of old photographs. One was of the building in question. A sign on the side of the building pointed to a door that led to the basement. The sign read, "Billiards."

Merrehope

*L*IKE many old mansions, Merrehope has a long history of numerous owners and occupants...which provides a fertile ground for hauntings. The twenty-room Greek Revival mansion began as a cottage built on property given by Richard McLemore, Meridian's first settler, to his daughter, Juriah Jackson in 1859. The John Gary family bought the cottage in 1868 and added additional rooms. After the home changed hands several times, it was finally completed in 1904 by the S. H. Floyd family.

In the 1930s the mansion was divided into eight apartments, and these were rented into the 1960s. In 1968, the Meridian Restorations Foundation, Inc. purchased the home and began its restoration. Since it was opened to the public, Merrehope has served as the site for many Meridian social functions. But at least two of Merrehope's numerous visitors refuse to leave. One in particular, Eugenia, keeps a close check on Merrehope and the people who make the old mansion a part of their lives. Fonda Rush, president of the Meridian Restorations Foundation, has had a long relationship with Merrehope—and Eugenia.

"I've been involved with the house since the foundation bought it," Ms. Rush said. "And when I was in college, I would have dreams of Merrehope, and I dreamed something was calling me here. In fact, I was Merrehope's first tour hostess. But I didn't have any unusual experiences until the summer of 1973.

"At that time, I was dating a man in the Navy. I had been telling him about Merrehope and he wanted to see it, so we drove over one night. We were still furnishing the house, so there were no sheers on the draperies. He walked up on the front porch and I walked up on the side porch. When I walked around to him, he had a funny look on his face. He said, 'You scared me. I saw your reflection. When you walked across the porch, the light was shining behind you and it reflected. I saw your shadow and I thought someone was in the house.'

"I said, 'You couldn't have seen my reflection. There's no light over there.' Then we *both* looked through the windows and saw Eugenia standing in the center of the hall! She looked like a solid figure. She was wearing an 1860s-style outfit with a hoopskirt. The top was a solid green and the bottom was a greenish plaid. Her hair was pulled back.

"It scared us to death. It seemed as though she was aware of us and was watching us as we were watching her. We ran back to the car and drove to my mother's house, went in and sat on the couch. My mother looked at us and laughingly said, 'You two look as though you've seen a ghost.' That was the first time I saw Eugenia." But not the last.

Several weeks later, Ms. Rush was working at Merrehope when one of the ladies involved in the restoration said, "Fonda, I want to show you something the Gary family gave us." She showed Ms. Rush portraits of two young women.

"I knew immediately when I saw the portraits that one of them was the woman I had seen a couple of weeks ago," Ms. Rush said. "But for a long time, I didn't tell anyone. It's just easier not to tell."

The portraits were of the two Gary daughters. Both Eugenia Gary and her sister died before the family moved from Livingston, Alabama, to Meridian. Neither sister ever lived at Merrehope.

One incident Ms. Rush experienced still leaves her puzzled, even though it happened almost twenty years ago. "It is as clear to me as the day it happened," she said. "One summer day, I went upstairs and was standing in front of the bay window in the Bride's room. I looked down and

Since one of Eugenia's favorite pastimes seems to be gazing out an upstairs window, even passersby have seen glimpses of her. Merrehope—Front view.

"It scared us to death. It seemed as though she was aware of us and was watching us as we were watching her." Merrehope—Display in bride's room.

saw Union soldiers in front of the house! It was a Cavalry. They began moving toward the house and the next thing I remember, I was in the basement. I don't know how I got there. I'm sure I walked, but I don't remember the transition. I remember feeling the sensation of having to hide."

Merrehope was used as the headquarters for two Confederate generals during the Civil War. Even though no records indicate occupation by Union forces, Merrehope was almost the only structure to survive the Union onslaught. It seems reasonable to assume that as soon as the Confederate soldiers evacuated Merrehope, the Union soldiers moved in. Ms. Rush feels she was tapping into someone's memory. But whose? Eugenia did not live at Merrehope during the war. And the scenery outside the window was similar to that surrounding Merrehope.

Shelba Inman, Ms. Rush's sister, is a hostess at Merrehope and lives in an apartment which is a part of the mansion. She has also had experiences with Eugenia which date back for many years. "Once my sister was visiting a friend in the apartment where I now live," she said. "My boyfriend and I were walking in the garden at the side of the house. We saw a faint light and the figure of a woman going back and forth between the windows on the second floor. Both of us saw it. I've never seen her since then, but I've felt her. She checks up on me when I'm sick."

Eugenia isn't the only permanent resident at Merrehope. Ms. Rush believes the ghost of a former teacher who committed suicide in a bedroom on the second floor still haunts the scene of his death.

"He put whiskey bottles on the mantel in his room, shot off all the bottles, and then turned the gun on himself," Ms. Rush said. "You can still see where the bullet holes in the mantel have been repaired. When the foundation bought the house, the room was just as it was when he died. The bottles were still there; the bullet holes were still in the mantel.

"He doesn't seem to roam very much. Eugenia wanders throughout the mansion, but the man doesn't. I have smelled cigarette or cigar smoke in his former room and no one has smoked in the house since the foundation bought it.

"Our workers have come in contact with the male ghost. They were doing some plaster work when they heard a crashing glass sound. They thought their ladder had fallen on a window and broken it. They ran and looked but could never find anything.

"And the footsteps we hear from this room are heavier than those we hear in the rest of the house," she said. "Sometimes the footsteps are so heavy that the prisms on the chandeliers dance."

Many of the ladies who work at Merrehope have had ghostly experiences. "Sometimes we hear talking and think someone is in the next room," Ms. Rush said, "but when we check, no one is ever there. And we hear a lot of knocking sounds, like someone is at the door. Also, several people have seen dark shadows walking behind them."

Tourists occasionally get a taste of the supernatural. Several have asked why they feel a cold spot beneath Eugenia's portrait. And one particular incident with a tourist convinced Fonda Rush that Eugenia was real—not just a manifestation of an overactive imagination.

"I was giving a tour to about five or six ladies," Ms. Rush remembered. "One of the ladies asked if her mother could speak to me after everyone else had left. I said 'yes' and looked over at the woman. She seemed concerned or upset. I couldn't imagine what she was so upset about.

"She said, 'Ms. Rush, you have two ghosts in your house. One is a man and one is a woman.' I was surprised because we don't mention them to anyone."

Since one of Eugenia's favorite pastimes seems to be gazing out an upstairs window, even passersby have seen glimpses of her. A young man who lives in the neighborhood was passing by the house late one night with a friend.

"I saw Eugenia in a downstairs window," he said. "She was dressed in an old-fashioned white dress. She looked very real, but I knew she wasn't. I asked my friend if he saw her and he said, 'Yes.'"

It wasn't the first appearance Eugenia had put in that night. At a Merrehope party earlier that evening, Sara Rush was standing on the porch. "I saw Eugenia standing inside looking out the window at me," she said. "Later the same night, I saw her again. I was upstairs alone and I looked through the sitting room...she was standing in the bathroom facing me."

Ms. Rush said Eugenia seems to be especially active when there is a lot of activity in the house. She remembered one particular night during the annual Trees of Christmas event at Merrehope. "A friend and I were closing. In the past, I had told her some of my stories and she had laughed. We began hearing footsteps upstairs. That's not uncommon...we hear footsteps all of the time...people walking, constantly walking.

"At the time, though, ghosts didn't enter my mind, because I thought the steps were outside and someone was walking on the porch. Then the steps got closer. I got scared and my friend said, 'Someone is hiding in the house.' I said, 'I don't know. It could just be the ghost.'

"She started laughing and said, 'There's no ghost. Call the police.'

"We were going to wait at the front door for the police and run outside when they got there. Then she said, 'I'm going upstairs and see who it is.'

"By this time I was really frightened because I thought it was possible that someone was hiding up there. And besides, all of the upstairs lights were off. I said, 'We don't need to go up there.'

"She said, 'I'm going up.' She got a pair of scissors for a weapon and said, 'If I yell, you go on outside and don't worry about me.'

"In less than a minute, I heard a yell and she came running down the stairs. She hit the door and was outside before I was. When we got outside, the police still weren't there, so we sat in her car.

"I asked her what happened, but she wouldn't tell me. She only said, 'Fonda, I will *never* doubt your ghost stories again!'"

Harry's House

WHEN Roger and Ruth Howell chose a site for their new home in 1977, they picked a heavily wooded setting in the Lake Serene area of Hattiesburg. The contemporary ranch-style home fronts a quiet lake. At its back lie gently rolling forests thick with pine trees. The peaceful setting gives no hint of the tragedy which took place on the site back in the fall of 1959.

As Roger Howell worked on his property, establishing lawns and gardens and clearing paths through the woods, he began discovering chunks of metal. As a pilot, Mr. Howell immediately recognized them as parts of an airplane. Curious, he began asking questions around town and discovered that a secret military aircraft, a B-58 jet bomber, had crashed on his property on October 18, 1959. The plane carried a three-man crew, two of whom ejected to safety. One however, a man named Harry Blosser, ejected too close to the ground and didn't survive. He was found near the crash site still strapped in his seat.

The Howells began to notice unusual things were happening around the house. Each morning when she left for work, Ruth Howell carefully locked all doors to the house. When she returned, the door to the laundry room would be unlocked. She would hear the door on the woodbox beside the fireplace open and close. On nights when she was alone, she would hear someone putting wood on the fire in the den. When she checked, she was alone in the silent house.

A variety of incidents continued. One night as Mrs. Howell and her son, Gary, watched television, they heard a loud "pop" in the kitchen. "We jumped up and ran in, but we couldn't find anything wrong," she remembered. "The next morning I opened a cabinet and found a large mixing bowl broken in half. The break was so smooth it looked as though someone had cut it with a glass cutter." No one had been in the cabinet and there were no temperature changes which could have explained the incident.

The Howells began to joke and say, "We must have a ghost. He must live in the attic and come down at night through the woodbox." Since they knew of the unfortunate Harry, they began to call the ghost "Harry."

Harry's antics got stranger. The Howells began to notice that when they went into the attic, things would break down...the refrigerator, washing machine, cars. Mrs. Howell decided to "appease" Harry. "The next time I had to go into the attic," she said, "I decided I would talk to Harry and tell him why I was there and that I didn't mean to harm or disturb him." Although she felt foolish talking to a ghost she really didn't believe existed, she was tired of things breaking down. It worked; nothing happened.

A week later Mr. Howell needed to go to the attic and Mrs. Howell reminded him to "talk to Harry." He just laughed and said, "You can't be serious. I'm not about to talk to Harry." The next morning the dishwasher broke.

Harry's strangest—and most costly—incident was a battle between the lawn tractor and Mrs. Howell's Cadillac. The Cadillac lost. Mrs. Howell remembered: "I came home from work and parked my car near the lawn tractor which had been sitting there for days. Later that night, our son Scott, heard the door from the rec room to the patio closing. He thought it was his dad. He heard the lawn tractor start but still didn't think anything was wrong. Then he heard the engine straining like it was against something and couldn't go any further." Scott was amazed to find that the tractor had run into the car, then turned and gone down its side

130

causing a long scrape.

Roger Howell, an engineer as well as a pilot, believed their dog must have jumped and accidentally hit the key. His wife disagreed for two reasons: "First, I never saw that tractor start without their having to try over and over again. Most of the time they would have to jump it off to get it started. Second, the lawn mower would not start in gear; you had to put it in neutral." Also, neither of the Howells can explain their dog's strange reaction that night.

The German shepherd was a devoted watchdog and guarded her master's property zealously. "No one came on our property without our knowledge," Mr. Howell remembered. Yet when the Howells ran outside to check the damage to their car, their loyal shepherd was lying on the patio with her paw over her eyes.

The insurance company had a difficult time accepting the Howells' explanation. Both are sure their claim became a joke around the insurance office. Roger Howell said, "They would call over and over, a different person each time. They would ask questions like 'Now, exactly what color was the tractor?' I could just see them laughing and deciding who would make the next call." Eventually, the insurance company's magazine published the incident under the heading, "You're not going to believe this one."

How does Ruth Howell explain the incident? "I have no explanation except someone had been in the attic shortly before."

The Howells believe Harry may have chosen them because they are a military family and he feels comfortable with them. Roger Howell was in the military and was a pilot, as is their oldest son. Their second and third sons were also connected with the military. And where was Harry during those years between the crash and the time the Howells built their house? "Looking for a home, I guess," smiled Ruth Howell.

"It was like a train or a storm had hit the house; it sounded like a bunch of shelves had fallen over and all the contents had hit the floor."

Sanctuary for a President

BEAUVOIR was the last home of Jefferson Davis, the only President of the Confederate States of America.

Built in 1852 by James Brown, a planter from Madison County, Beauvoir was originally named Orange Grove, and was intended for use as a summer home. After Brown's death, the house and its surrounding acreage were purchased by Sarah Dorsey, a widow and successful writer. She renamed the house "Beauvoir," which is French for "beautiful view."

Following the Civil War, Davis was imprisoned for two years at Fort Monroe, Virginia, by a vengeful North. After his release, Davis was a man without a country. The North had stripped him of his citizenship and northern businessmen used their influence to block his efforts to find gainful employment. Davis and his family wandered for almost ten years—to Canada, Cuba, New Orleans, England, and Memphis—as Davis searched for a way to support his family.

In the mid-1870s, Davis finally decided he was ready to write the book he had promised himself he would write—a book detailing the years of the Confederacy. He began searching for a place where he and his family could live in peace—a place that would afford him the solitude he needed to write. Mrs. Dorsey, who had been a friend for many years, invited him to visit Beauvoir. The house and its beautiful surroundings delighted him, and he was soon hard at work on *The Rise and Fall of the Confederate Government.*

132

Some people have recently claimed to see a figure at the rear of the house late at night—a figure in a tall hat and frock coat walking in the rose garden.
Beauvoir—Side view.

Mrs. Dorsey realized that Jefferson Davis had found a haven—where he could be content and could come to grips with the immense tragedy in which he had been a major player. She sold him Beauvoir for $5,000 in February of 1879. Even though Davis was still a man without a country, he was no longer a man without a home.

After Davis died in 1889, his wife, Varina Howell Davis, moved to New York City. In 1906, she sold Beauvoir to the Mississippi Division of the Sons of Confederate Veterans for the token sum of $10,000. She stipulated that the house be a shrine to the memory of Jefferson Davis, and the surrounding grounds be operated by the state as a Confederate Soldiers' home.

Veterans and their widows lived at Beauvoir until 1957. When the property was no longer needed for their care, total control returned to the Mississippi Division of the Sons of Confederate Veterans.

Today, the Mississippi Division of the Sons of Confederate Veterans continues to operate Beauvoir as a shrine to the only President of the Confederacy. An arch presented by the United Daughters of the Confederacy in 1917 stands at the entrance to the grounds. Its inscription reads: "Stranger tread lightly here for this is holy ground." But not just strangers tread lightly around Beauvoir, for in addition to being holy ground, it seems to be *haunted* ground as well.

Colonel Newton Carr, Jr. was the superintendent at Beauvoir for eight years. "I witnessed very little," he said, "but I heard a lot.

"Before I got to Beauvoir, a hostess saw one of the busts shedding a tear late one afternoon just as they were about to close. And many people over the years claim to have seen Mr. and Mrs. Davis.

"While I was there, some of the employees said they felt the presence of Mr. Davis. They also said they would see him out of the corner of their eyes, but when they turned to face him, he would disappear.

"Some of our guards have witnessed the ghosts of old veterans," Colonel Carr continued. "But one night, it wasn't a ghost that frightened the guard. Somehow, an alligator had gotten in the lagoon and it honked and scared one of the guards to death. He didn't know what it was. And once he put the flashlight on him and saw a four-foot alligator staring at him, he was *really* scared.

"Like a lot of other people, I experienced cold areas all over the grounds—like I was feeling a *presence*," he said. "I'd be walking on the grounds on a hot summer night and get a chill by walking through a cold area. I'd walk through the area and the temperature would return to normal."

Some of the most interesting phenomena occur in the Hayes Cottage, one of two cottages that flank the main house. For years, Hayes Cottage served as a guest cottage for visitors. Colonel Carr vividly remembers one night he spent in the Hayes Cottage shortly before he became superintendent.

"I was watching television in the sitting room," he said. "It was about one-thirty in the morning when I heard a terrible noise. It was like a train or a storm had hit the house; it sounded like a bunch of shelves had fallen over and all the contents had hit the floor."

Colonel Carr jumped from his chair. "I looked everywhere inside. Then I took a flashlight and went outside—I knew that something had collapsed. I went all the way around the cottage, but I couldn't find a thing. It was so vivid—I can't believe I imagined it. Later, I was talking to a man who was on the board of directors at Beauvoir and he said the same thing had happened to him when he was sleeping in the bedroom." And during his tenure at Beauvoir, guests continued to have similar experiences.

Rex Wiseman, who was a frequent visitor to the cottage, had an experience he will never forget. "A friend and I would go down and open up the cottage together. I noticed he would always go into the closet and pull out the rollaway bed and set it up in the sitting room. I always thought it

"They would see him out of the corner of their eyes, but when they turned to face him, he would disappear." Jefferson Davis' Death Mask.

was strange that he would always give up the bed which was really nice—beautiful oak with posts that were nine or ten feet tall and hand-carved. Maybe he had a reason.

"One night, after midnight, my friend was asleep in another room on the rollaway bed. I suppose I had been asleep, but if I hadn't been asleep, I was at the dream stage where you drift off. Suddenly I heard a tremendous noise and felt the house move. I heard glass breaking and what sounded like timbers cracking. It reminded me of the time I was in a restaurant and a car ran into the side of the building. It scared me straight up out of the bed!

"I realized I was standing in the middle of the bedroom floor—just that quick. I reached over, turned the light on, grabbed a pistol and ran through the house. I knew a security guard patrolled at night and I thought, 'That damn fool has run into the side of the house.' I looked outside and didn't see anything. My second reaction was, 'Maybe the chimney has fallen on the house.'"

Mr. Wiseman woke his friend and ran outside. The friend followed asking, "What is going on?"

Instead of answering, Wiseman asked, "Man, what *was* that?" He replied, "What are you talking about?"

Wiseman answered, "There was one hell of a bang back there."

Wiseman was convinced the cottage had taken a direct hit from something. "I went all the way around the house. Remember now, I was in my skivvies with my pistol and a flashlight. I didn't see anything. I thought, 'Well, maybe a big tree limb has fallen on the house,' but I couldn't see anything.

"My heart was racing. I wasn't considering anything supernatural at the time. I was sure something had fallen from the sky—maybe something from an airplane—and hit the house. I told myself, 'I don't see it now, but in the morning when daylight comes, there will be a gaping hole somewhere.'

"I lay back down but didn't sleep very well that night.

The next morning, I went out and didn't see *anything*."

The following evening, Mr. Wiseman and his friend were sitting outside discussing the events of the night before. Colonel Carr joined them and Wiseman asked, "Did anybody report anything crazy last night?" Carr answered, "No, everything was real quiet." Wiseman said, "Well, something happened to me. I woke up when something hit this house—and hit it hard." "Really, why do you say that?" asked Carr. He replied, "It was so loud it really startled me," and repeated the events of the night before.

After listening quietly to Wiseman's story, Carr said, "You're not the first person to tell me that. Several people have reported the same thing." Then Carr related his own late-night experience in the Hayes Cottage.

Colonel Carr and Mr. Wiseman discussed a possible answer to the mystery at Hayes Cottage. A hurricane hit the Mississippi Gulf Coast in 1893. During the storm, a tree fell on the Hayes Cottage and destroyed the back of the cottage. Perhaps the house is remembering the fury of that night.

For most of the curious, however, the central question is, "Does Jefferson Davis' ghost walk at Beauvoir?" Perhaps. Some people have recently claimed to see a figure at the rear of the house late at night—a figure in a tall hat and frock coat walking in the rose garden. "I would hope Mr. Davis is still at Beauvoir," said one admirer. "I think that would be wonderful."

Afterword

I hope you enjoyed reading *Ghosts!* as much as I enjoyed writing it. I also hope your view of the supernatural has been broadened. From my own perspective—as I mentioned in the Foreword—doing the investigative work and research for *Ghosts!* was a truly enlightening experience. Even though each story I was told was unique, I quickly became aware that certain phenomena occurred at almost every site.

Most common was the sound of footsteps. And in some instances, where two or more ghosts are known to haunt the same house (such as at Merrehope), listeners can detect which ghost is on the prowl by the distinctive difference between the footsteps of the resident ghosts.

The number of people who reported hearing crashing noises was a surprise. We knew that at our studio, crashing sounds occur almost every day; but we had never thought they were a common paranormal phenomenon. Apparently we were wrong.

The large number of people who reported actually *seeing* ghosts was also a surprise. In the majority of stories in this book, someone, at some point, has seen a ghost. Some ghosts appeared as shadowy figures, but other ghosts, such as the ones at Twelve Oaks, have looked so real they have been mistaken for the living.

Many people, such as Carl and Dixie Butler of Temple Heights and the carpet layer at the Spengler Street Hotel, reported hearing voices coming from empty rooms. The voices sounded so real that the listeners never even considered the possibility that the voices didn't belong to living people...until they checked and realized the rooms were empty.

From blinking lights at Longwood to haunted stereo

equipment at Hilltop, flashing lights and other electrical disturbances are commonplace. In fact, the most unusual experience we had while researching this book involved both flashing lights and malfunctioning electrical equipment.

The flashing lights incident took place at Springfield, which Bob, Lee, Shellie and I always look forward to visiting. Arthur La Salle has been a friend for years and it is always a special treat to visit him. Of all the wonderful old mansions in this state, we have a special feeling for Springfield. I knew from previous conversations with Arthur that he had experienced some unusual phenomena at Springfield, so when Bob and I started planning this book, we arranged to get together. Arthur suggested we come one evening after the daily tours were over.

It was a beautiful summer night with fireflies flitting all around us. We sat on the porch in Arthur's comfortable rockers until long after dark. The mosquitoes chased us inside and we went to Arthur's study. We talked about his unusual experiences before we went on to other subjects.

We hadn't discussed ghosts or psychic phenomena for at least an hour when the clock struck nine. Bob said, "We'd better go; it's been a long day." The four of us stood...and every light in the house went off. I don't know how long they stayed off, a few seconds probably, but long enough for me to think, "Wow, it's so dark in here it's like when the lights are turned off in a cave." They came on...and went off again. They flashed a total of three times. We looked at each other and Arthur said, "The electric company must be having problems." I thought, "Sure they are." As soon as we reached our hotel, I turned on my tape recorder and asked Shellie to relate what had happened when the lights went off. Shellie, who thought the whole experience was "neat," happily obliged. I held the recorder for her as she spoke, and I interrupted her once to ask, "And then what happened?" When she finished, I turned off the recorder.

I usually record interviews when they are to be used for

publication, since I don't want to risk misquoting someone. I had used the tape recorder all day and had even used it at Arthur's when we discussed incidents I knew I would be writing about. The next day, I used the recorder again.

When I began transcribing my tapes from the Natchez area, I found that the tapes were all perfect...until I got to Shellie's description of the flashing lights. At that point, her voice on the tape speeded up so much that I couldn't understand a word she said—sort of like a "Chipmunk's" voice except much faster. The only part of the conversation that was normal was when I asked, "And then what happened?" But when Shellie continued, again her voice was so distorted it sounded like it was being run at a fast-forward speed.

I don't understand how the tape recorder could have malfunctioned. It only has one speed and is either on or off. Everything I had taped earlier that day was fine as was everything I taped the following day. It's another incident I have no explanation for.

Other strange incidents followed us in our travels. Sometimes it seemed as though the ghosts themselves were aware we planned to visit—at several locations people mentioned a sharp increase in paranormal activity in the days preceeding our arrival. Footsteps, for instance, often increased in intensity and frequency.

While I have described various phenomena which occurred frequently, I must also mention that there are several types of phenomena which we did *not* encounter in our research. Most books about ghosts seem to emphasize unearthly screams and moans and rattling chains—but in our travels, we encountered very few stories of screams and moans...and not a single rattling chain! Maybe our Mississippi ghosts are just more civilized and cultured, but theatrical moans and clamorous chain-dragging do not seem to be big in their arsenals of paranormal display.

One of the greatest pleasures in writing this book was visiting the places where supernatural phenomena have recently been encountered. One of the criteria for the stories I included was, in fact, that they be stories of ongoing experiences with the unknown. I chose to exclude those in which phenomena did not extend into the present day, even when the stories were well-known or had been passed down in families for generations. Many of the old homes we included welcome the public at least part of the year, usually during pilgrimages. Some are bed and breakfasts. A few, such as Springfield, Stanton Hall, Cedar Grove, Beauvoir, and Waverly are open year-round. You yourself may wish to visit some of these places. If you have any doubt as to whether or not a home is open, contact the tourist bureau or chamber of commerce of the town in which the house is located.

And if you *do* go looking for ghosts either in the places we visited which are open to the public, or in a "haunt" of your own choosing, where should you look? Here's a clue: after looking at the photographs in this book, you may notice there are quite a few pictures of halls and stairs. In many instances, Bob has photographed the areas where the phenomena most often actually occur; and with striking regularity, those areas are halls and stairways. The only explanation Bob has is that, "Stairways and hallways are places of transition. If you are on a stairway or in a hall, you're leaving one place and going to another." How that ties in with ghosts, I'm not exactly sure, but ghosts seem to be spotted most often on stairs and in halls.

Finally, I leave you to judge for yourself whether ghosts are real. But even if you don't believe in them, you may do well to exercise caution when touring antebellum homes. You may do well to give an ear to voices that speak to you in southern accents from empty rooms. You may do well to heed warnings from strangers standing by Mississippi roadsides. And even though most of our Mississippi ghosts seem to be friendly, you may do well to follow the lead of the eighteenth-century French noblewoman Marie Anne du Deffand. When asked whether she believed in ghosts, she replied, "No—but I'm afraid of them!"

Acknowledgments

No book can be produced by the efforts of only one or two people, and this book is no exception. We are very grateful to the people whose stories appear in this book. They generously gave us their time and shared their wonderful stories with us. Without them, there would have been no book.

We are also grateful to our children, Lee and Shellie. They spent many days traveling with us and helping carry heavy bags of equipment through scorching heat, pouring rain, and freezing wind.

Dozens of people scouted stories for us. Some stories are in this book and some are not, mainly due to a lack of time and space, but we thank each person who took the time to help us.

A very special thanks must go to Linda Mann, Carolyn Denton, Connie Taunton, Janice Heindl, and Lenore Barkley. I don't think we could have done this book without your help. You all deserve a medal for the jobs you do.

Thanks are also due to Barney and Gwen McKee, who were almost as excited about this book as we were—you've been great to work with!